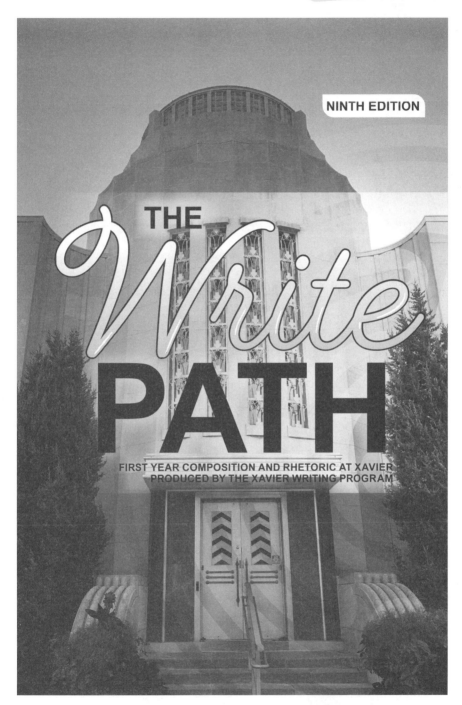

NINTH EDITION

THE *Write* PATH

FIRST YEAR COMPOSITION AND RHETORIC AT XAVIER
PRODUCED BY THE XAVIER WRITING PROGRAM

VAN-GRINER
LEARNING

The Write Path

First Year Composition and Rhetoric at Xavier
Produced by the Xavier Writing Program
Ninth Edition

Printed in the United States of America
10 9 8 7 6 5 4 3 2 1
ISBN: 978-1-64565-470-4

Van-Griner Learning
Cincinnati, Ohio
www.van-griner.com

President: Dreis Van Landuyt
Senior Project Manager: Maria Walterbusch
Customer Care Lead: Lauren Wendel

Frey 65-470-4 Su24
334452
Copyright © 2025

Table of Contents

Editor

Renea C. Frey, PhD.

Editorial Assistants

Kelly Austin
Matt Cummings
Marty Dubecky
Izzy Maffetone
Maggie Myers
Megan Nieto
Lisa Ottum
Rita Rozzi
Sheena Steckl

Acknowledgments

I would like to thank Xavier's English Department, the Writing Center, and the College of Arts and Sciences Dean's office for supporting this project. I would also like to thank Kelly Austin, Matt Cummings, Marty Dubecky, Izzy Maffetone, Maggie Myers, Megan Nieto, Lisa Ottum. Rita Rozzi, and Sheena Steckl for their time judging entries and giving input about our students' writing. Perhaps most importantly, thanks to all of the student writers from ENGL 101 and 115 who submitted work to make this publication possible and to the faculty who teach first-year writing, supporting and challenging Xavier students to become the best writers they can be.

Welcome!

As first year writers at Xavier, you may have questions or concerns about writing in your college courses. You may love to write and be excited about the new forms of composing you will learn in college or in your major, or you may feel intimidated and uncertain about what to expect. This book is designed to give you more information about writing in college and offer some examples of what successful college-level writing looks like, straight from Xavier students themselves.

In the first section of this book, you will find information about terms, ideas, and practices that will help you succeed with college-level writing and orient you to practices, policies, and resources for writing here at Xavier. As you read, you may find that you have heard some of this information before, though some of it may be entirely new. Words such as *rough draft, peer response,* and *rhetorical appeals* are likely to play a big part in your writing process in college, so being familiar with the meanings of these words can help you find your way in your writing courses. Additionally, this text will cover issues of academic honesty, plagiarism, and how to properly cite sources in research-based writing so that you can create quality work that acknowledges information you have learned from outside sources. Resources such as the Writing Center and the library will also be explained so that you know where to turn when you need additional support and information for your writing.

In the second section, you can read selected essays from first-year students at Xavier who, like you, were recently in ENGL 101 or ENGL 115 working on similar assignments. Looking through their work, you can see what type of writing is expected so that you can better understand the genres you will be asked to write in your first-year writing courses. You may have seen some of these before—such as a research-based argument—but you will be prompted to examine the writing more deeply with questions at the end so that you can more fully appreciate the "how" and "what" of research writing. Other genres—such as the rhetorical analysis or multimodal argument—may be less familiar, and seeing examples can give you an idea of what to expect from these assignments. These examples are not meant to be copied, nor do they represent a rigid set of expectations for an assignment, but rather, offer a model of one way that this type of writing can be successfully crafted.

As you write papers in your ENGL 101 or 115 courses, be on the lookout for papers you wrote particularly well, and consider submitting them for consideration for the D'Artagnan Award and next year's *The Write Path* publication. By submitting your work, you can support and encourage students who, like you, will be first-year college writers next year. What you learn now can benefit your fellow students in the future, so please pass along your wisdom and work.

Everyone arrives at college with different backgrounds, experiences, and types of education. This book has been created to help put you on the "write path" in your first year as a Xavier student and to answer questions you may have about writing in college. Also, if there is anything that would have benefited you that was not included in this book, please let me know so that we can consider including it next year. Good luck in your first-year writing classes!

Sincerely,
Dr. Renea Frey
Writing Program Director

Introduction to The Write Path

College Writing—What Makes It Different?

Nearly everyone does some sort of writing in high school, but what kind and how much work you do may vary greatly. In your first year of college, one of the educational goals is to give all students a solid, common foundation in particular subjects, including writing, which can help you for the rest of the time you are at Xavier.

A common genre that students often learn in high school is the five-paragraph essay. While many of the conventions for this type of writing may transfer to college writing, you will also be expected to move beyond the five-paragraph essay to write increasingly complex, longer assignments. In many cases, you will be building upon writing skills you have already learned in high school and expanding them to fulfill new, more in-depth writing prompts.

For instance, you will still need to make strong, focused thesis statements that give the reader an overview of the claims you will be making, and then organize the rest of your paper around supporting that claim with evidence. In most cases, you will also include elements like topic sentences that announce the content of a paragraph and transitions that allow the reader to easily follow your thought process. You should have a strong conclusion that gives the reader a "call to action," identifies the larger implications of your work, or clarifies why thinking about this issue or text in this way matters. While many of these conventions may be similar to what you have done in high school, it is likely that your instructors in college will ask for greater detail, more depth, additional outside sources, and longer length papers than you typically worked on in high school.

Some other differences in college writing include the following:

- The type of evidence that "counts" in some assignments may include peer-reviewed scholarly sources which are written by and for academics in specific disciplines. These pieces may be longer than popular articles, include more field-specific jargon, and be challenging to interpret for those who are new to a discipline.
- You will likely need to offer multiple perspectives in your work, including counter-arguments to your position or refutations of competing perspectives. It is not enough to only argue *your* side—you need to view and fairly represent issues from multiple positions.
- In some cases, you may be asked to write from a formal third-person perspective, but in other cases, such as narratives or reflections, you may have to write in first-person, beginning your thoughts with "I."
- You will likely write for different audiences, some of which may be a community of scholars, whereas other times, you may be writing for the public. You may also compose texts in multiple mediums, thinking about visual, textual, and sound-based approaches to reach diverse audiences.

- Different disciplines have different conventions, citation systems (e.g., MLA, Chicago, or APA), and expectations. As you write for different courses from across the university, you will find that writing varies between disciplines and that what counts as "good writing" may vary in each class.
- How you conduct research, integrate quotes, and cite sources in your work may be more rigorous than what was expected in high school. As you enter college-level work, you become a part of a community of scholars who have high standards for academic integrity and attribution for work and ideas. (More on this topic later …)

Even if you found writing in high school easy, the writing (and thinking) you will do in college will expand your previous skills. In addition, you will be writing for new audiences, about novel topics, and be asked to engage in assignments that will likely push beyond the work you did in high school. This learning can be both challenging and exciting, and the work you do in your first-year writing courses serves as a foundation for the writing you will create during your entire time at Xavier.

Process Writing

How many of us have waited to start a writing assignment until the night before, and then frantically written all night, quickly proofread the paper once or twice, and then turned it in at the last minute? While this may succeed in "getting the work done," few people (despite the claims every instructor hears) actually produce their best work under these circumstances.

A common practice in ENGL 101 and 115 courses will be to engage in process-based writing. In this approach, instead of writing assignments where you write on your own, turn in your writing, and then receive a grade, you will work on your writing gradually, in stages, with feedback from peers and/or your instructor at multiple points along the way. In many of your other courses, you will still be asked to create writing where the final *product* is what counts, but in your first-year writing courses, we will also focus on the *process*.

Some of you may already be familiar with peer review—sharing your work with classmates to receive feedback and suggestions for revision—but in first-year writing, this may be more directed and involve particular practices, such as reading out loud, filling out a worksheet based upon the writing you read, or writing a reflection about what you changed in response to your peer's suggestions. In addition, you may receive feedback from your instructor at various points in your composing process or be asked to submit a proposal, outline, or research plan for your projects. By focusing on the process, your instructor can guide you as you draft, review, revise, redraft, and revise your papers again.

A process-based approach to writing may include all or some of the following steps:

- Invention work, including brainstorming, heuristics, listing, free-writing, or other exercises to start your thinking about a topic
- Proposals or research plans that ask for details about what, how, and when you intend to create a project

- Annotated bibliographies which require you to document, summarize, and analyze the sources you are exploring for your research
- Exploratory Essays (sometimes called Synthesis Essays) may be assigned which will ask you to discuss all of the sources you have examined for your research, and reflect upon how what you have learned informs your thinking about your topic.
- Outlines or zero drafts where you begin the initial stages of your paper but have not yet composed a full copy
- Rough or first drafts that include all of your completed ideas but that are not yet in the "polished" stage of drafting
- Final or polished drafts that represent your best work which has been revised, edited, and proofread after receiving input from peers, your instructor, and/or the Writing Center
- Reflections on your writing process, revisions, or finished work

Throughout this process, your instructor may choose various places to intervene, read your current work, and offer feedback or direction. Your peers, too, may be a part of this process, in both formal peer reviews and informal discussions in class. Unlike many of your other courses, your instructor may give you points along the way for different stages of drafting—your finished paper may not be the only writing that "counts" toward your grade.

For many reasons, it is important to keep up with this process as it is outlined in your class schedule. First, it may affect the grade you receive on the overall assignment, especially if various drafts have point values assigned to them. Second, in a course that utilizes peer review, it is important that everyone have a draft to share so that participation is fair and possible. Third, by receiving feedback along the way, you can be more confident that you are fulfilling the assignment correctly and change course sooner if you find that you are not. Lastly, composing your work in steps, even if it is unfamiliar to you, will give you new, valuable skills that you can use in other courses.

Though many students can get into the habit of writing their entire paper quickly the night before, to succeed in college-level writing, it is imperative to take more time planning, drafting, and revising your work. Even the very best writers who are accustomed to receiving A's for their work can benefit from feedback and revision. Additionally, as you progress in your college education, you will encounter assignments that simply cannot be completed in one or two sittings. In order to produce your best work, as well as reduce needless stress, it is important to get into the habit of working on writing assignments in stages, over time.

When we "re-vise," we are actually "re-visioning" or "re-seeing" our work with fresh eyes. If writing assignments are put off until the last minute, there simply is no time to do this, nor is there space to receive feedback, visit the Writing Center, or read work out loud in order to catch errors in wording.

For these reasons, your first-year writing courses will engage writing as process in some manner. This may be a new approach, or it may simply expand your past experiences. Either way, learning to see writing as an ongoing process will save you time, stress, and disappointment in the long run, and support your work in other courses. ENGL 101 and 115 encourage a foundation for best practices in writing that will serve you throughout your college career and beyond.

Jesuit Education and Principles

As you were preparing to come to college at Xavier, you probably heard about—or perhaps already knew—that a Jesuit education adheres to principles that may be different from the focus of other institutions. There are certain values that Jesuit institutions hold in common, which can be interpreted as "invitations," rather than a list of prescribed rules. While there may be some variation or interpretations in how these ideas are applied, they generally include the following:[1]

- **Reflection** invites us to pause and think deeply about the circumstances in our lives and the world in order to be more self-aware and socially conscious.
- **Discernment** invites us to make decisions using a range of feedback sources, such as rational, affective, and transcendent/spiritual, in order to make choices and take action that will contribute good to our lives and the world around us.
- **Solidarity and Kinship** invites us to connect with and learn from others in a spirt of unity, care, and mutual regard.
- **Service Rooted in Justice and Love** invites us to invest our lives into the well-being of our neighbors, particularly those who suffer injustice.
- **Cura Personalis,** or "care for the whole person," invites us to care for others while recognizing the uniqueness and wholeness of each person.
- **Magis** invites us to ask, "Where is the more universal good?" when making decisions and invites us to produce the best quality of work possible in order to be the best we can **be.**

These values combine with a specific approach to teaching found at Jesuit institutions and form the basis of the educational experience at Xavier. You may hear this method referred to as "Ignatian pedagogy," which is named after the founder of the Jesuit Order, St. Ignatius, where "pedagogy" refers to a theory of teaching and learning. This system relies upon a more reflective and recursive way of learning, where students are asked

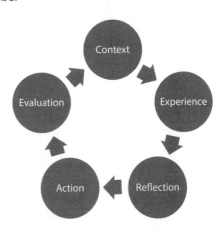

---

[1] Descriptions are taken from the "Xavier Values" page under Xavier's Mission on the Mission and Identity website, as well as information in Canvas about Jesuit Icons provided by Instructional Design.

to acknowledge and examine the context(s) in which they find themselves or encounter issues, incorporate and understand their own experience, reflect upon, question, and learn from what they see in the world around them in order to take action, whereupon they evaluate this process, including the effectiveness of their actions, and begin again.

As you can see, this is not a passive approach to learning where a professor transfers knowledge to students who then repeat back what they have learned. Instead, this type of education anticipates active involvement from students where they are constantly reflecting upon what they see, hear, and learn in order to make good choices that are in alignment with their values and goals. Hopefully, those goals will likewise be in alignment with the greater good, so that as students move through their educations and lives, the world is made a better and better place for all who dwell within it.

While these may seem like lofty goals for a first-year writing class, the values of a Jesuit education and Xavier's Mission are well-known across campus and will likely inform many of the assignments, topics, and writing that you undertake while in your classes. Being aware of these values as the foundation of Xavier and its approach to teaching and learning can help you more deeply invest in your own commitments as you move through your classes. Reflecting on where you come from, who you are, what troubles the world around you, or what creates injustices for yourself or others is often a great place to start when seeking a topic for the various papers you will undoubtedly encounter in your first-year writing courses. Using your ability to reflect, discern, and perceive your life as interacting with others in a spirit of solidarity and kinship may help you find meaningful ways to apply and develop your rhetorical skills in your first-year writing classes by seeking topics that are truly meaningful to you and help serve the greater good. In this way, you may benefit both yourself and others around you as you develop your writing skills in the spirit of *eloquentia perfecta*, or communicating skillfully in order to serve the greater good.

Rhetoric and Rhetorical Theory

You have likely heard the word "rhetoric" many times in your life, often in a derogatory manner that implies "merely words" or words without honesty or substance. Rhetoric, which will be addressed in both ENGL 101 and 115, is actually the art of speaking and writing effectively that dates back at least as far as ancient Athens in the Western tradition. Aristotle described rhetoric as "the faculty of discovering in any particular case all of the available means of persuasion" and this definition, or similar ones offered by Cicero, Quintilian, Augustine, and others, points to the study of rhetoric as the analysis and use of words to persuade an audience.

The ability to persuade effectively has implications for the use of that power, so some rhetoricians also address the idea of *ethics* within or alongside rhetoric. In the Jesuit educational system, there is a tradition called *eloquentia perfecta*, which is speaking (or writing) well for the greater good. As you study, analyze, and effectively use rhetoric, keep in mind that rhetoric, like many tools, can be utilized in both ethical and unethical ways. As you build knowledge and become more aware of rhetoric in the world around you, recall the practices of *reflection* and *discernment* that are also part of the Jesuit tradition—when you make choices about using your rhetorical skills, remember that rhetoric can serve the greater good or merely be self-serving.

Though we may not be aware of it, we use and encounter rhetoric all the time in our daily lives. You might engage rhetorical means when you try to persuade your roommate to pick up her dirty socks, convince your parents to support a trip abroad, or write a cover letter to apply for a new job or internship. In each of these situations, you use persuasion to try to convince an audience of your perspective. Conversely, you also encounter rhetoric everyday in magazine or online ads, opinion pieces in the school newspaper, or political speeches on television or the Internet. Even memes, by using stock images and brief lines of text, provide short arguments that make a claim and try to convince the viewer of a particular perspective.

Because we use and encounter rhetoric so often in our everyday lives, it is important to understand how it operates in order to use it effectively and ethically. It is also crucial to recognize how rhetoric works on *you* in your daily encounters with texts, people, and ideas. With knowledge of how rhetorical appeals work, you will be able to engage the world around you with greater discernment, which will allow you to make more informed choices about the arguments you regularly witness.

Rhetorical Terms and Appeals

In ENGL 101 and 115 you will likely learn about *rhetorical appeals,* or the specific ways that people are generally persuaded. There are three main appeals:

- *Ethos*: The character or authority of the speaker/writer, which includes the reasons you might trust what a particular person says, either because of her virtues or knowledge. Audiences are not persuaded by speakers they do not trust.
- *Logos*: This is the logic or reason behind an argument that appeals to our rationality. An argument has to make sense and be backed with evidence in order for it to be accepted by an audience.
- *Pathos*: The emotions we feel when faced with a situation can also affect our choices and beliefs. We may be moved by compassion or fear to take a certain action for a social cause, or may feel joy and fulfillment when we are convinced to spend the weekend on vacation with friends.

Ideally, all of these appeals will work together in well-constructed, logical arguments that speak to our values and are presented to us by ethical, knowledgeable people. As you can imagine though, this is not always the case, which is why it is so important to discern and identify rhetorical appeals in our everyday lives.

Other terms you may hear in your studies of rhetoric include the following:

- *Audience:* All rhetorical acts engage a rhetor and an audience to whom the rhetor speaks or writes. You already tailor your messages depending upon your audience whether you are aware of it or not. When writing rhetorically, you will make more conscious choices about wording, style, or method of delivery in order to reach your audience most effectively.
- *Purpose:* All communication has a distinct and specific purpose. Do you want your audience to take a particular action? Or believe a new idea? Knowing what you want to accomplish with your writing will help you craft more effective texts.
- *Kairos:* This refers to the timing of a rhetorical text—what is relevant today may no longer make sense three months from now. A rhetorically effective text will take into account the timing of events and will arise at the proper moment.
- *Exigence:* Rhetorical texts respond to stimuli or events and may pose a potential solution to a problem. The exigence is a state that demands attention, and the rhetorical text is what arises in response to it.
- *The Five Canons of Rhetoric*
  1. *Invention*: Pre-writing work such as brainstorming, heuristics, listing, etc., that allows you to "discover" your argument
  2. *Arrangement:* Putting together your argument in a logical, effective way that your audience can easily follow
  3. *Style:* May include the wording, tone, or appearance appropriate for your text, audience, and purpose
  4. *Memory:* In classical rhetoric, this refers to memorizing a speech, but today it can indicate referencing citations, digital memory, or public/cultural memory that influences rhetorical texts.
  5. *Delivery:* For classic oratory, this might include gestures or tone of voice, but in written texts may refer to the way writing is presented on a page, digital delivery, or forms such as video or podcasts.

Knowing these terms and understanding their application will give you a vocabulary to analyze, think, and write about the way rhetoric works. In ENGL 101 and 115, you will likely conduct a *rhetorical analysis* at some point, which will ask you to examine a text and analyze its rhetorical components. You may also be asked to consciously utilize rhetorical appeals in your own writing as a means of creating more effective arguments. These may be new genres of writing and examples of effective rhetorical analyses, and rhetorically grounded arguments will be offered later in this book.

Though you may not have realized it, you are already surrounded by rhetoric and confront rhetorical appeals everyday. By understanding how rhetoric operates, you will be able to identify the persuasive tactics you encounter in order to make more informed choices *and* to interrogate your own use of rhetoric to ensure that your rhetorical skills are used in a way that serves your values.

Language, Power, and Inclusivity

Rhetoric, as stated earlier, can be a tool of power—the power to persuade, change policies, alter perceptions or beliefs—and as such can either challenge or support injustice. Language itself also reflects the ideologies from which it springs, so that what we think of as "proper English" is actually a specific dialect spoken by those in the highest tiers of power. This dialect is often called "Standard English" (SE) but contemporary linguists also use the term "White Mainstream English" to highlight the racial systems that inform this standard. While people in fields like linguistics and rhetoric may be aware of these conversations and the justice-based challenges to language bias, in other fields there is little conversation about, or challenges to, entrenched conventions and expectations that privilege particular dialects over others.

The Xavier Writing Program is committed to challenging linguistic bias and racist practices by acknowledging that multiple dialects are equally relevant and that students have a right to their own language practices. When approaching issues of dialect in your college writing, it may be helpful to consider both your own position and language, as well as the position and language of those you hope to persuade. This may also be a conversation to have with your professors, especially when you have rhetorical reasons for choosing to write in a particular voice for certain projects. There are no easy answers to negotiating language conventions and expectations, but open dialog and discussion of these practices, as well as challenging areas where injustices have traditionally occurred, is an important step in the process of social justice.

Our identities can be very tied to the language and words we use, as well as the labels others use for and with us. The Xavier Writing Program is likewise committed to being sure that our students feel welcome in the classroom and that their professors respect their identities. If you have a name that is different from the class roster, please advise your professor at the beginning of the semester so that they can make a note of this in their records. Faculty at Xavier should also be happy to use the pronouns with which you identify, so please let them know what pronouns to use when talking or referring to you. Some people choose to do this by adding signature lines to their emails that indicate their pronouns, or you can tell your professor at the beginning of the term (or even before by contacting them via email) so that you know your identity is welcomed and included in your classroom spaces.

The Xavier Writing Program is dedicated to the principle of *cura personalis* (care of the whole person) and making our classrooms and learning materials accessible to our students. Everyone comes into the classroom with different abilities, learning styles, backgrounds, experiences, and goals. If at any time you find that you would learn better in a different way or that course materials are confusing or difficult to find, please talk to your instructor.[2] Similarly, if you

---

[2] Any students who feel they may need an accommodation based on the impact of a documented disability should notify the course instructor and contact Cassandra Jones in the Learning Assistance Center at 513-745-3280 or e-mail jonesc20@xavier.edu to coordinate accommodations.

find you are struggling in areas in or outside of the classroom, having trouble coping, or keeping up with your work due to mental health concerns, please talk to your instructor, who may be able to offer you ways to navigate classroom issues and/or point you toward resources available to you on campus.[3] College can be both an exciting and stressful time, and as part of the Xavier community, we are invested in the idea that we look out for one another and reach out when we need help.

Creating an inclusive environment where everyone is welcome and feels a sense of belonging requires us all to communicate clearly, compassionately, and ethically and is in alignment with both Xavier's Mission Statement and the principles of *eloquentia perfecta*. Part of what makes an education at Xavier different from other institutions is the centrality of the principles of a Jesuit education, which ask us to care for one another, live in solidarity and kinship with and for others, and to be—or become—the best versions of ourselves through education, reflection, discernment, and a commitment to justice. Inclusivity and participation by all students in our first-year writing classes is a foundational place to put these values into action, and as such, the Xavier Writing Program is committed to supporting these principles.

Research, Citation, and Academic Honesty

In college, you will be asked to write research papers in many of your classes. In ENGL 101 and 115, you will learn about the conventions of research and citation as part of your course work. Again, some of this may be review, but many students find that college-level research writing entails more careful documentation than their high school writing required.

Research can be viewed as an ongoing conversation between multiple parties within and across disciplines. As new ideas are discovered, academics write up their findings and publish them in scholarly journals, where they are reviewed by their peers. When you read scholarly articles, you are "listening" to those conversations, and when you write research papers, you are "joining" that conversation by synthesizing information and applying it to your own interests.

One way that you can start to understand and analyze this scholarly conversation more thoroughly is through creating an Annotated Bibliography as part of your research work. Although what is expected for this assignment will vary depending upon the course, discipline, parameters of the upcoming paper you may write, concepts covered in class, or the preferences of your professor, all annotated bibliographies serve the purpose of both *summarizing* and *analyzing* the specific sources you are exploring in your research process. In addition to demonstrating to your professor that you are actively engaging with research on your topic, creating an annotated bibliography also allows you to contemplate sources more deeply, analyze their position or content, and consider how each source contributes to the work you are doing yourself. This thinking and writing

---

[3] Find out more at http://www.xavier.edu/health-wellness/counseling/index.cfm and http://www.xavier.edu/psychologicalservices/welcome.cfm or by calling (513) 745-3022 for McGrath or (513) 745-3531 for Psychological Services Center.

process can be very beneficial to you as you conduct research, allowing you to pause and think critically about each source that you examine prior to using it in a research paper or other assignment.

For an Annotated Bibliography like this, you would list each source alphabetically by author in proper citation format (MLA 9th edition for English classes, but check with your professor if you are unsure or if you are working on an assignment in a different discipline), and then provide the annotation—a summary and analysis of the source—underneath the entry. If you receive an Annotated Bibliography as an assignment, be sure to check with your professor about the expectations for each entry and how it should be formatted, as this can vary greatly depending upon the course. Remember, too, that this kind of assignment is something you can take to the Writing Center for additional feedback or help with citation methods.

Because scholarly writing depends so much on the ongoing research "conversation," the academic community has very high standards for crediting and citing research that others have conducted. While standards for citing and incorporating sources into your own work may vary in high school, once you are in college, there are particular rules that you must follow in order to keep your writing and research practices ethical.

In college, you will likely be asked to integrate outside research with your own ideas. When you do this, you may make claims or express ideas that are yours, and then back them up with evidence that comes from outside sources. This is a more complicated process than, say, writing a research report that summarizes the ideas of someone else or an opinion paper that simply expresses your own position. In college writing, you will often be asked to integrate both of these practices into a more complex written argument.

When you utilize research conducted by others, it is important to always attribute those ideas to their sources. There are a variety of ways that you might incorporate outside sources into your work including the following:

- *Quote:* A short passage that is written out word for word exactly as the original author stated it
- *Paraphrase:* A segment of someone else's work that you have put into your own words
- *Summary:* Condensing the overall idea of a work into a much shorter format in your own words

To maintain academic honesty, you must cite the sources you use in all three of these cases.

Citing a source typically includes in-text citations inside of parentheses at the end of the sentence where the outside source is quoted, paraphrased, or summarized. For MLA format, which you will use in most of your English classes, this will include the author's last name and the page number of the article or book where you found the information. Your papers should always include a Works Cited page where you list all of the sources you used for your paper, arranged alphabetically by the author's last name; this should also include important publishing information, which will be covered in your class or found in an MLA 9th edition style guide.

Please note that as of April 2021, MLA has moved to 9th edition style guidelines, so the information in your textbook may not be updated if you are using an edition published prior to that time. You may need to consult an online database such as Purdue Owl, or purchase an MLA update supplement for your textbook. Check with your professor to see which style guidelines they prefer.

Your ENGL 101 or 115 instructor will go over proper citation formats in class for different types of documents, but the first and most important step is to remember that you *must cite these sources,* even if you do not quote them directly. Although you may lose points for formatting a citation incorrectly or need to revise if you've made a mistake, citing outside work in the first place will allow you to avoid charges of plagiarism or academic dishonesty, which are much more serious.

Avoiding Plagiarism

Plagiarism can be defined as using someone else's words or ideas without properly identifying the source. Plagiarism can carry dire consequences for students who engage in it, including failing grades for the assignment or course and in some cases, suspension.[4] Here are some basic types of plagiarism that can compromise a student's academic integrity:

- *Intentional Misrepresentation:* This occurs when a student deliberately attempts to present another's work as his or her own. This can include copying or paraphrasing someone else's writing without attributing the source, buying a paper online, or having someone else write the paper.
- *Self-Plagiarism:* This type of misrepresentation happens when a student "recycles" a paper written previously for another class or context. In some cases, you may want to continue research that you have conducted for another class or project, but *you may not use any writing that you have already turned in* for a grade. If you decide to further previous research, it is best to check with your instructor and be totally honest about what you are doing so that your motives and writing process are completely transparent.
- *Unintentional Misrepresentation:* When a student is not familiar with community citation standards or that these standards may be different from what he or she did in high school, it is possible to plagiarize due to uncertainty or lack of knowledge. When in doubt, cite your sources.
- *Patchwriting*: Rebecca Moore Howard (1993) defines "patchwriting" as *"copying from a source text and then deleting some words, altering grammatical structures, or plugging in one-for-one synonym-substitutes."* This type of plagiarism is not always the result of dishonesty; sometimes

---

[4] For more information about plagiarism and academic integrity, please see the Xavier Library's resource, "Plagiarism for Students: Understanding and Avoiding."

it occurs because students are not familiar with the ideas or language they are attempting to incorporate. Nevertheless, it is still considered plagiarism *even if the sources are cited.*

- *Excessive Quotation:* Even if you cite your sources, you cannot cobble together a paper based mostly upon the words or ideas of others. When you use long quotes, do so sparingly and only when the author has stated an idea in such a way that it warrants the in-depth use of another's specific words. (Also check MLA citation guidelines, as long quotes require block formatting that is different from short quotes.) Be wary, however, about using multiple sets of long quotes as this may border on plagiarism, even if you cite the sources. When you write papers in college, the bulk of the words and ideas should be your own.

In some cases, you may not need to cite a source. For instance, when referring to your own personal experiences or thoughts, original research you have conducted yourself, or when you use common knowledge or widely accepted facts, a source is not necessary. What constitutes "common knowledge" may vary widely but is generally considered to be a fact that is easily accessible and consistent across many sources (e.g., the Declaration of Independence was ratified in 1776). However, if you are not sure if your information is considered common knowledge, *cite the source.*

Integrating sources correctly into your own work will also help you to avoid plagiarism, as doing so allows you to clearly show in your writing which ideas are your own and which ideas come from others. Although you may understand how a source supports or more fully clarifies your own work, it is important to explicitly explain that to your audience. Framing outside information will make your work more effective and also help you avoid accidental plagiarism:

- *Introduce* the integrated work with a short sentence or phrase that contextualizes the information for your reader.
- *Quote, Paraphrase, or Summarize* the work, including proper in-text documentation per citation style and then including all sources used in your Works Cited page.
- *Comment* on the work and how it relates to the argument or information you are presenting. This will help your reader understand how you interpret the work you are citing and its relationship to your own ideas.

Learning to effectively and ethically integrate research into your own writing is a key component of what you will learn in ENGL 101 and 115—skills that will also support your success in other classes throughout your time as a student. While other disciplines may use different citation styles (such as APA or Chicago), all disciplines value honest, ethical research practices and eschew anything that could be construed as plagiarism or misappropriation of another's work. For these reasons, it is very important that you learn and understand the research and citation methods expected of you in college, as the consequences for not following these community standards can be dire with long-term effects on your academic career.

Consequences for Academic Dishonesty

Your instructor will have a clearly stated plagiarism policy in your ENGL 101 or 115 syllabus, and you should understand thoroughly the possible ramifications for not properly attributing your sources. Plagiarism often occurs when a student is pressed for time or overwhelmed by an assignment; sometimes, an otherwise honest student may make unfortunate choices in high pressure situations that lead to more work, trouble, and upset than taking the time to do the work honestly. If you find yourself in a situation where you are stuck or afraid that you cannot complete the work on time, talk to your instructor, or take your assignment prompt to the Writing Center for help or clarification. Even requesting an extension or having points docked for turning in a paper late is much less severe than a charge of plagiarism.

Students can mistakenly believe that their instructors will not know if they have plagiarized or copied a paper—in full or in part—from another source, but this is rarely the case. Software such as Turnitin catches many cases of plagiarism, and instructors generally know the writing styles of their students. With Internet technology, it is very easy for instructors to search for key terms in their students' work to see if a paper has been plagiarized or recycled from another source. Even under situations of stress, it is never a good idea to turn in work that is not fully your own—an honestly but poorly written draft can be corrected and recovered from, whereas an academic dishonesty charge will follow you throughout your college career.

Xavier's Academic Honesty Policy states the following:

> The pursuit of truth demands high standards of personal honesty. Academic and professional life requires a trust based upon integrity of the written and spoken word. Accordingly, violations of certain standards of ethical behavior will not be tolerated at Xavier University. These include theft, cheating, plagiarism, unauthorized assistance in assignments and tests, unauthorized copying of computer software, the falsification of results and material submitted in reports or admission and registration documents, and the falsification of any academic record including letters of recommendation.

> All work submitted for academic evaluation must be the student's own. Certainly, the activities of other scholars will influence all students. However, the direct and unattributed use of another's efforts is prohibited as is the use of any work untruthfully submitted as one's own.

> Penalties for violations of this policy may include one or more of the following: a zero for that assignment or test, an "F" in the course, and expulsion from the University. The dean of the college in which the student is enrolled is to be informed in writing of all such incidents, though the teacher has full authority to assign the grade for the assignment, test, or course. If disputes of interpretation arise, the student, faculty member, and chair should attempt to resolve the difficulty. If this is unsatisfactory, the dean will rule in the matter. As a final appeal, the academic vice president will call a committee of tenured faculty for the purpose of making a final determination.

Please note that not only are there immediate consequences for academic dishonesty (including a zero for the assignment, an "F" for the course, or expulsion from the University), but also that this action will be reported to the Dean's office of the college in which you are enrolled, and that a record of this action will be recorded. While the ramifications for *any* instance of academic dishonesty are definitely not worth the risk, in the case of a second or repeated offense, the consequences are typically much more severe.

In all cases, academic honesty and integrity are always the "write path" to take. Citing your sources clearly and integrating them effectively into your own work will make you a better writer *and* help ensure your acceptance into a community of scholars.

AI in the Writing Classroom

You have probably heard quite a bit about artificial intelligence, or AI, over the past months. ChatGPT and other programs like it have been making headlines recently for its ability to produce writing and for educators' concern over possible plagiarism, so it is important for you to be aware of potential benefits and risks of these programs, along with what to expect from your professors.

AI like ChatGPT has the ability to revolutionize the ways that we write. While it is important to practice your own writing skills, there are many ways to use these tools that you might find very helpful when working on your assignments. For instance, AI can help you to brainstorm and fine tune your ideas to create an outline to assist you in clarifying your thoughts, and it may be useful when reviewing your work for grammar, style, and tone of voice.

However, it is important to remember that your professors will expect you to do your own writing and that these AI programs are still in development, and therefore, not always the most reliable. If you are planning to use ChatGPT or other language learning models, you should keep in mind the following:

- *Fake Information:* ChatGPT has been known to provide information that is factually inaccurate.
- *Citation Limitations:* ChatGPT and other programs often produce incorrectly formatted citations and can misattribute information to the wrong author. ChatGPT has also been known to completely bypass citing any of its information.
- *Hidden Biases:* AI often mimics harmful prejudices and biases that it encounters from information it pulls from the internet.

Finally, you should always keep in mind Xavier's policies on academic honesty when using programs like ChatGPT. The Xavier Writing Program recognizes both the benefits and risks of using AI to support the development of writing skills, as well as concerns over academic integrity. Additionally, we also recognize that copying work produced by ChatGPT does not help you to develop your writing, meet course goals, or internalize the information from class. You should also know that the university does not accept plagiarized work. While every department might have a slightly different approach to handling AI, here are some basic guidelines to help you determine how, or if, to use ChatGPT:

- *Check the Professor's Syllabus:* Every professor should articulate their expectations for use of ChatGPT and other AI programs in their syllabus. If you have any further questions, don't be afraid to ask your professor to clarify.
- *Check Assignment Rubrics:* Some professors might allow, or even encourage, use of AI for some of their assignments, while other assignments might require that you not use it, so always check individual rubrics. For ENGL 101 and ENGL 115, there are some writing assignments that require personal narrative components or ask you to reflect upon your experience writing. A personal story or reflection shouldn't utilize AI since that is specifically asking for your own experiences. On the other hand, the research paper might benefit from a brainstorming session with ChatGPT. Check in with your professor if you have any questions about when it may be an appropriate time to use ChatGPT.
- *Recognize AI is a Potentially Flawed Resource:* Due to the risks and limitations, ChatGPT and other programs will not always give you accurate information. Before using any information from these sources, always verify that the facts are correct.
- *Be transparent:* If you aren't sure how or if you are allowed to use AI on an assignment, talk with your professor. It is important to never try to pass off work as your own if it is not, and each professor may have very different ideas about acceptable usage of AI. When in doubt, ask.

Remember, too, that evaluating sources is an important part of the research process. *Always cite your sources,* which includes the use of AI tools. If you have checked the course syllabus and your professor's policy regarding AI, the assignment rubric, and verified the information, you may be able to use ChatGPT as a source. As with any source, it is necessary that you cite it in order to avoid plagiarism. For most English courses, you will be using the MLA citation style, which has recommended that you cite ChatGPT on your works cited page as, "'Description of prompt given to ai.' Prompt. *ChatGPT,* version, OpenAI, date, URL." The MLA (Modern Language Association) has also recommended that you treat ChatGPT as a third-party. In other words, try to track down the original source of the information if possible and give credit to that person. For instance, if ChatGPT gives you a statistic or quote that you want to use, identify where it originally came from in your writing by introducing the original author and stating that they were quoted in ChatGPT. You can find more information about citation expectations through the MLA's website. Remember that other departments might expect your citations to be completed using another style, so always check before you turn in an assignment. Also, keep in mind that these citations might change over time due to how new these developments in AI are.

Even when it is acceptable or helpful to use ChatGPT and other programs like it, *do not overuse these programs.* These tools should not be used as a replacement for your own writing and learning. As discussed above, there may be potential benefits to using AI but these programs, like all of your sources, should only be used to support your argument and help you through the writing process. Trying to pass off an AI generated paper as your own is a violation of Xavier's Academic Honesty Policy. Excessive use of quotes or patchwriting, even if it is cited, might also be grounds for plagiarism, depending on your professor's policy. If you are feeling unsure about your use of ChatGPT, you can always reach out to your professor for further guidance.

Ultimately, the decision of whether or not to use ChatGPT or related programs is up to your professor's policy and your discretion but remember to follow these guidelines and to always keep in mind the potential risks of using AI. Also, be aware that failing to cite the program and overuse of AI might result in a charge of plagiarism, so be careful about how you choose to incorporate AI into your writing. Remember that the goal of your first-year writing course is to develop your own voice and skill as a writer, and while AI may be used ethically as a tool to develop those skills, it should never be considered a substitute for learning, practicing, and developing your own voice.

Resources for Students

Xavier University McDonald Memorial Library

We often think of the library as a place to go to find books, but the library actually offers many more services that will be of use to you as you research various projects. In addition to the books housed in the library, you can also use OhioLINK or Inter-Library Loan (ILL) to check out any book available in libraries across the state or country. This gives you access to many more books than could be contained in a single building on campus. Keep in mind, though, that these services may take a few days to process your request and get the book to Xavier for you to pick up, so always start your research process early.

In addition to traditional print books, the library offers services to connect Xavier students to a variety of journals, media, and other resources. By using Search @ XU and the research databases, you can easily access thousands of resources, including scholarly journal articles. In ENGL 101 or 115, your class may take a trip to the library, or a librarian may come to your class to talk with you about how to search the databases and find the information you need. In an online course or remote learning environment, a librarian may videoconference with your class or you individually to provide research help. You can also drop by the library, call, or email the librarians to ask questions or to seek help if you are having trouble finding information.

The library has a makerspace on the first floor, right as you come in the main entrance from the Academic Mall. The makerspace is open to all students to explore, design, create, build, and collaborate using technologies such as 3D printing, circuitry, programming, a laser etcher, tools, arts and crafts, a Cricut, and more.

In addition to the library services, you can also use the Conaton Learning Commons (connected to the library building) as a place to study or meet with classmates to work on group projects. There are 12 group study rooms in the CLC with capacities that range from two or three people, up to 10 people. Many of these rooms are equipped with white boards or plasma screen projectors with web access, so you can easily share your work and collaborate in these spaces. There are also two small computing labs with access to photocopiers, printers, scanners, and computer workstations. Other student support services in the Conaton Learning Commons include Accessibility and Disability Resources, Math Lab, Writing Center, Language Resource Center, Student Success Center, Academic Advising, and Digital Media Lab. All of these services are here for you to use and can help support your writing and research in a variety of courses.

For more information and to get started with your research, visit the library's website at www.xavier.edu/library.

James A. Glenn Writing Center

The Writing Center is another important resource for students at Xavier to help them develop writing skills and to support them with writing assignments in various classes. Located in the CLC 400 (overlooking the circulation desk), the Writing Center offers peer tutoring help with writing during any part of the drafting process. While this is a great place to come if you want someone else to look over your paper once you have a rough draft, the Writing Center tutors can also help you understand an assignment more fully before you start drafting, work with brainstorming ideas, give assistance organizing a paper, offer direction if you are halfway through an essay and get stuck, or provide information about documenting sources. At any stage of the drafting process, the Writing Center is an invaluable asset for students working on writing.

If you use the Writing Center, it is best to make an appointment by emailing (writingcenter@xavier.edu) or calling (513-745-2875) since there may or may not be a tutor available if you just walk in. While the majority of students go to the Writing Center in person, sessions can also be conducted via video meetings or email. In the event of remote learning semesters, the Center will provide all sessions online.

When you go, be prepared with your assignment prompt and name of the class and professor, as well as any notes, drafts, or outlines you have already done. Think about areas where you need the most help with the assignment and have questions ready to ask the tutor, as this will allow you to make the best use of your time. It is optimal to plan to go to the Writing Center a few days before an assignment is due so that you have time to make revisions, or even do additional research before turning in work for your class. Sessions last about fifty minutes and the Writing Center is open a variety of hours (including Sundays) so that it is possible to find time in your schedule to make an appointment.

Some students mistakenly believe that the Writing Center is only used by people who struggle with writing or who are "bad" writers. The truth is, no matter how skilled a writer you are, receiving feedback on what you have written can improve the overall quality of the work you turn in. Everyone benefits from having reviews of their writing, and almost all writing can be developed more fully. The Writing Center is a key support service for success in ENGL 101 and 115, as well as other courses and projects that require writing. Be sure to utilize this resource while you are at Xavier.

Online Access

In most of your first-year writing classes, instructors will make use of an online Learning Management System (LMS) called Canvas, which you can access through various devices, whether you are on campus or off. While instructors may use the services provided in Canvas differently, you should be able to find many of your learning materials in this online interface, including the syllabus, assignments, links, readings, and course policies. Your instructors may provide you with these materials in class and/or in hardcopy formats, too, so be sure to check with your instructor about how Canvas is used in your particular class. Canvas provides an easy way for students and instructors to access course materials and assignments, turn in work, have text-based class discussions, or meet virtually in video conferences via the Teams interface. Your instructor may choose to use some or all of these tools even when meeting face-to-face on campus. You can find more help with Canvas at this link on Xavier's site, including information on the computer specifications to run Canvas: *https://www.xavier.edu/ts/students/canvas-for-students-9914*.

Some Words About Success

In your first year at Xavier, you will be building the skills you need to succeed in your classes, as well as your life beyond the university. The writing you will practice in your ENGL 101 and 115 courses is a part of that skillset, but it does not exist in isolation. Part of success in writing—or college, or life in general—is planning your time wisely so that you are able to meet all of your commitments without being overwhelmed or stressed in the process. It may be a change for you to have to plan so many activities, assignments, and classes yourself, but learning to do so effectively will ensure that you are able to be successful in your courses.

Success in your first-year writing course is strongly tied to success in college overall, which is yet another reason to commit to coming to class and producing the best work you can in ENGL 101 and 115. At Xavier and many other institutions, students who persist in their first-year writing classes are more likely to stay in college and complete their degrees. First-year writing courses give you the foundational skills to write effectively for an academic-level audience that will help you succeed in your other classes and beyond as you move into your chosen career. Additionally, at Xavier (and most other institutions) first-year writing is a requirement for graduation, so it is important to take this course seriously and attend class during every scheduled meeting, prepared and ready to participate fully with your classmates.

Because so much of the learning in ENGL 101 and 115 takes place in the classroom amidst interactions with peers and professors, attendance in first-year writing courses is mandatory. Your individual professor and the Writing Program have specific policies about late work, tardiness, and attendance that you must follow in order to succeed, which you can find in the syllabus for your class. It is not possible to learn the material in ENGL 101 or 115 and successfully integrate the Learning Outcomes without attending class, thus you cannot pass first-year writing if you have too many absences.

Learning to write well takes practice, which is why we promote a process-based approach to writing. You may find writing more challenging in college than you did in high school, but as with learning any new skill, you will find that you develop efficacy the more you practice. Be sure to give yourself enough time to work on your writing assignments, even in courses where the process itself is not emphasized as much as it is in ENGL 101 or 115. Brainstorm, jot down outlines, take good notes on your research, write rough drafts, and visit the Writing Center. All of these practices will not only increase the likelihood of achieving higher grades on your papers, but also develop the skills you need to write well in all areas of your life.

Remember though, as with any skill, writing capability is acquired over time and with repeated practice. While feedback from peers, your professor, or a peer tutor can aid in developing your skills as a writer, these practices do not automatically guarantee that you will get the highest grade possible on an assignment. All students build competency over time, and peers, professors, and tutors can only address a few issues at once. Be patient with the process and engage all of the resources available to you at Xavier to ensure that you reach the highest level of writing success you can during your time in college.

Student Work

How to Use This Text

In the upcoming pages, you will find examples of student work from first year students who, just like you, took ENGL 101 and/or 115. These examples can be used in a variety of ways and are here to support the writing that you will do in your first year at Xavier.

One way that these student essays can help you is to illustrate what the different genres of writing you may encounter in ENGL 101 and 115 look like. It can be hard to craft a particular kind of writing, such as a rhetorical analysis or multimodal argument if you have no idea what these genres are or should include. By looking at an example, you can see what typically goes into creating this type of work, as well as observe how this can be done particularly well.

These papers and multimodal compositions do not serve as a rigid template for you to copy. Rather, you should use these texts as models for what to expect in a particular genre, what you should include, what "works" about a piece of writing, and then consider how you can adapt or include those skills in your own work. By "stepping back" from a text and asking questions about how it is composed, you can analyze not only the content, but also the rhetorical and compositional strategies that are employed in creating that piece of writing.

To guide you through reading these examples, each paper or multimodal project will be foregrounded by a reflection from the students themselves, discussing their writing process for that assignment. You can see through their words what challenges, obstacles, strategies, and steps they took to get to the finished piece that is published in this book. As readers, we often only get to see the product of a writer's efforts, but in this text, you will also gain insight about the process that led to these essays and projects. By reading these reflections by students, you might find that you relate to some of their struggles, or learn an important tip that could help you with your own writing.

After the reflection you will find the essay itself (or a link to a website in the case of some multimodal compositions) followed by a short series of questions. These questions ask you to look more deeply at the work itself, to ascertain what you think the writer was doing or intending at different points along the way. How does this writer transition from one idea to the next? What kinds of sources does this writer use as support for her argument? How are quotes integrated into this argument? How might multiples modes of communication, such as images, text, or sound work to create an overall message? These are the kinds of questions that may be presented after the essay itself, for you to consider and/or for your instructor to use in class to prompt discussion about the writing process.

By examining the projects and essays of other students who were working under similar conditions, you can seek guidance and encouragement for your own work in first year composition and rhetoric courses at Xavier. Additionally, by analyzing the composing process in this way, you can learn more about the way that you write. How do *you* transition between ideas? Support your claims? Or integrate quotes? By getting into the habit of analyzing writing itself, rather than only its content, you gain *meta-cognitive awareness* of your own writing process. By understanding how writing and composition happen, you can acquire insight about what you do, how you do it, and why.

This knowledge can allow you to make more conscious choices and utilize the Jesuit principles of *reflection* and *discernment*. Through reflection on your writing, you can learn more about yourself as a writer and communicator, and then make more discerning choices about those practices. As you develop your skills as a writer in your first-year courses, you will build the foundation of your future academic success, as well as establish tools with which to participate in your communities, careers, and civic lives.

This text is designed to assist you in those endeavors and to serve as a guide for your first year as a college writer.

The D'Artagnan Award

The essays that you find in this book all come from entries for the D'Artagnan Award, an annual award co-sponsored by Xavier's Writing Program, the Dean's office, and the Writing Center. Each year, students are encouraged to submit their best work from ENGL 101 and 115 for this award. The submitted essays can be written in any genre, and the top three winners, along with a selection of other exemplary student work, will be published in *The Write Path: First Year Composition and Rhetoric at Xavier* for the following year.

The name for this award was chosen specifically because D'Artagnan, like our first-year writers, had to work hard to improve his skills, overcome obstacles, and rise to the challenge of new situations that require maturity and development. First-year students who win this award become leaders for future students, as their work will become a tool to guide new first-year writers on their educational journey.

The D'Artagnan Insignia: Advocacy in Action

As you go through the student work in the next section, you will see that some of the essays have an insignia next to them featuring a silhouette of D'Artagnan. The D'Artagnan Insignia for Advocacy in Action indicates work that speaks to social justice issues and writes in the true spirt of *eloquentia perfecta*, or "speaking well for the greater good." The work with this insignia meets the criteria for this distinction as it challenges the roots of inequality in our world, utilizes student writing talents to further the work of social justice, and gives voice and consideration to perspectives that are often suppressed. Even in your first-year writing, there may be times when you can use your communication skills in this way, to promote the greater good, and to offer viewpoints that will allow your reader to consider issues from a new standpoint. The Xavier Writing Program believes that this is an important use of student writing, so when you see this insignia, it may be an opportunity to listen, pay attention to the voices speaking, and consider how these ideas might support a campus and world that are more justice-based and inclusive.

As you use this text this year and develop your writing skills in ENGL 101 and 115, please consider submitting your favorite pieces for next year's D'Artagnan Award. You can learn more about this award and submit work anytime throughout the year at https://www.xavier.edu/english-department/dartagnan-award/index.

Category: Research-Based Argument

Research-based arguments are a staple of college writing. In many of your classes, you will be asked to conduct research on a topic, form a position, and then compose a formal argument that weaves together reliable evidence with your own ideas. There are many ways to approach research-based argumentation, such as Classical or Rogerian arguments, and several sub-genres or types of arguments you may be asked to compose, such as proposal arguments (which argue for a solution to a problem) or rebuttals (which ask you to argue a different side from an extant source), as well as many others. In all of these cases, you will need to conduct research, form a position, solution, or claim based upon that research, and then logically organize your ideas while also acknowledging that there are positions other than your own.

Our featured essays all address matters of ethics, equity, autonomy, and justice and cover a wide range of topics. Additionally, several of them carry the D'Artagnan Insignia for Advocacy in Action due to the focus on social justice that these authors decided to explore. These essays offer effectively argued perspectives on subjects ranging from physician-assisted death, abuses of the troubled teen industry, the controversial practice of banning books in schools, and addressing systemic racism that will offer readers well-informed information on important issues, as well as provide models for effective college-level writing.

Our D'Artagnan Award winner for Research-Based Argument is Summer Wolf for her essay "How Different Factors of Physician-Assisted Death Affect Its Ethical Nature." Taking an inquiry-based approach, Summer researched a topic that was of importance to her major and future career, exploring this complicated issue in order to form a position, which she shares in her essay. Our readers noted that her evidence was strong, that she employs a variety of rhetorical appeals, and that her counterargument is clear and well-integrated. Readers were also impressed with her mindful treatment of a difficult topic, noting that "this is a controversial issue but the student writer did a great job of handling ethical concerns sensitively."

The second essay in the category of Research-Based Argument is by Bryn Powers, who asks in her provocative title, "Troubled Teens or Teens in Trouble?" This essay, which carries the D'Artagnan Insignia for Advocacy in Action, explores the troubled teen industry, which promises to help young people who are struggling emotionally or behaviorally, but instead abuses and isolates them. Readers commented that Bryn's essay on this disturbing industry is "very persuasive and reads like a journalistic exposé," a genre that helps expose abuses that might otherwise go undetected by most. Her research-based argument brings awareness and offers a warning for those who might turn to these services, not understanding the true nature of their practices.

"The Need for All Books in School" by Gillian Ocampo addresses the issue of book banning in schools from multiple perspectives. Utilizing subheadings to organize her argument, readers thought that Gillian's essay was well organized, easy to follow, and that they "enjoyed the conversational nature of this piece—it felt like reading a published article in a magazine and has a wide audience appeal." Because of Gillian's focus on the importance of keeping books in school that support minority perspectives that are often suppressed, this essay was also selected for the D'Artagnan Insignia for Advocacy in Action.

Our fourth essay, "Institutionalized Racism—A Call for Change," is by Destiny Starks. This far-reaching argument explains the history of racism in America, points out many sites of continued racism today, and argues for policy, representational, and educational solutions. Readers said that Destiny's claim was clear and specific and that she did an excellent job of organizing a lot of information about a complex issue in a way that made the argument easy to follow for readers. They also commented on her "thoughtful and thorough engagement with counterargument" and noted that "this writer takes on a huge issue and tries to give workable solutions." Because of its extended engagement with social justice, this essay was also chosen for the D'Artagnan Insignia for Advocacy in Action

Although you may find that your classes require you to write different types of Research-Based Arguments, or that your prompts differ from the ones for which these essays were written, there are many elements you will see in these essays that will help you with your assignments. When reading the essays, notice how the writer sets up their argument. What background information is given? How does the writer clearly state and refer back to their thesis? What kinds of evidence do these writers use? How does the writer deal with counterarguments? Are claims and refutations dealt with sequentially or are they interwoven? How does the paper conclude? What does the writer leave you wanting to feel, believe, think, or do?

In all of these cases, students have produced exemplary work in their first-year writing courses and learned skills for research writing and argumentation that will serve them in other courses. Although each discipline has its own set of rules and expectations for writing, many of these skills—such as integrating sources, making claims, using evidence to support one's position, etc.—will be necessary in a variety of contexts and for multiple of your future courses. Your first-year writing classes will help you develop these skills more fully so that you are able to utilize them effectively throughout your time at Xavier.

How Different Factors of Physician-Assisted Death Affect Its Ethical Nature

Summer Wolf
D'Artagnan Award Winner for Research-Based Argument

Reflection

When my teacher first told our class about the English 101 Inquiry-Based Research Project, I almost broke the one rule we had in the class—"do not panic." The paper had to be somewhere from five to ten pages long, approaching our topics from a neutral standpoint while using rhetorical appeals to emphasize the importance of our topics. The project consisted of a peer review and a working draft, ending with a final draft which was to be turned in at the end of the semester. For this type of project, it is common to feel overwhelmed and stressed about the amount of writing and research that must be put into it, as well as keeping good quality writing consistent throughout the paper. For me, the most important part was choosing a topic that not only was something I was interested in and would be beneficial for me to know more about, but also a topic in need of more accessible insight. To determine this, I thought about my career in nursing and controversial topics within the field. I also thought about which topics are over-discussed or strongly emotionally charged. This led me to physician-assisted suicide.

Throughout my paper, I carefully deliberated every rhetorical decision I made while considering my audience, families and healthcare providers of PAS patients. I utilized the techniques we studied previously in the semester, taking inspiration from the Rhetorical Analysis assignment. Doing this is the BEST advice I can offer to anyone writing a similar paper. Taking into consideration the exigence and public discourse of your topic and then applying the proper rhetorical appeals is essential to how effectively your text will resonate with your audience. An example of how I did this is when I changed the term "physician-assisted suicide" to "physician-assisted death." I made this decision because I did not like the feelings surrounding the term "suicide" and did not think it accurately represented the practice. Ensuring that you can approach your paper from an open-minded perspective is also vital to the writing process. Through utilizing this approach, I was able to produce a text that I am extremely proud of and hope can be used to assist future students through this project.

How Different Factors of Physician-Assisted Death Affect Its Ethical Nature

Imagine a 45-year-old mother of three, who has been diagnosed with and fought stage four pancreatic cancer for almost one year. She lives in a hospital, and can hardly get out of bed to hug her children. The mental, physical, and financial strain her sickness has put on her entire family is catastrophic. Her doctor has given her a prognosis that she will not live longer than two more months, and those months will be filled with painful treatment and drug regimens. The woman decides she wishes to utilize the option of physician-assisted death, and is allowed to die with dignity and control over her life.

The concept of physician-assisted death, otherwise referred to as PAD, is an important but controversial topic within the medical community regarding the ethical nature of certain practices. PAD has been a consistently and strongly argued topic, with medical backing in some areas, and emotional backing in others. Critics tend to bring religion, politics, and alternative care methods as their main reasonings; however, they sometimes fail to investigate those claims fully. There also tends to be a strong misinterpretation of the term physician-assisted death, with the press and media spreading that incorrect use of the word further. Although the practice is almost entirely referred to as physician-assisted suicide, this is an inaccurate representation of the practice, insinuating that the patients are committing a form of suicide rather than taking control over their inevitable death. Because of this, the practice will be referred to as physician-assisted death. PAD has a strong foundation, existing to offer alternatives to those who have terminal diseases and short remaining life expectancies, and is based on the principles of "autonomy, beneficence, nonmaleficence, and justice" (Benedict 1). Physician-assisted death is a necessary and ethical practice, following strict criteria and requirements, ensuring that autonomy is respected and honored, and giving control and comfort to patients regarding their end-of-life care.

Many individuals who oppose the practice of physician-assisted death believe that "artificially terminating the life of a human is an unethical act even though there is any rationale or motivation by the person requesting euthanasia" (Lee 95). This opinion is fueled mostly by misinformation regarding PAD spread by the public, media, press, and academic literature. They make the mistake of using the terms euthanasia and physician-assisted death, also known as death with dignity, which can be an unintentional misspeak with big consequences. Even though physician-assisted death is technically a subdivision of euthanasia, the latter word is too broad to grasp the true meaning of physician-assisted death. Euthanasia "refers to an act of dying that is peaceful, comfortable and painless," but it is not specific to terminally ill patients. This is a key component of physician-assisted death, being that it is only available to terminally ill patients with a prognosis of less than six months. It is important that, when advocating for physician-assisted death, those who favor the practice differentiate it from homicide or euthanasia, and recognize that the practice is in association with life-ending diseases.

Understanding the criteria that must be met for patients to be eligible for physician-assisted death is essential to forming an educated opinion on the practice. Per U.S. legislation, "all [laws] require that patients requesting physician-assisted death satisfy three criteria: (1) terminal illness through a prognosis of having 6 months or less to live, (2) competence and intact judgment, and (3) voluntariness" (National 9). The first requirement, that the patient has a terminal illness with less than 6 months to live, ensures that this practice is only being used with patients who will die eventually regardless. This also ensures that PAD not be abused by mentally unstable or suicidal patients, who aim to use the practice as a form of self-inflicted death. Competence and intact judgment greatly simplify the reality of the patient's mental state; however, as long as healthcare providers (HCPs) can tell the patient is requesting the service of their own free will, they will meet the criteria for competence. The last part of the criteria, voluntariness, ensures that the patient is not forced or coerced into the practice by a family member or peer. These factors are of paramount importance, especially in maintaining the dignity and autonomy of the patient.

The objectionary party of the physician-assisted death discourse has argued that "the fear of losing autonomy at the end of life seems to be a main rationale driving many terminal patients to seek PAS" (Merrell). This statement, in simplified terms, explains that rather than autonomy being an advantage for patients at the end of their lives, it pushes them to choose PAD as a treatment, just so they can exercise a small amount of the control they have left over their lives. This argument is not sustainable due to the number of "procedural and administrative hurdles" patients must overcome before they can request PAD. An example of this is in Oregon, where the law states that (1) the patient makes two verbal requests, which are at least fifteen days from each other, (2) a written and signed request is submitted to the physician, which has been witnessed by at least two other people, (3) two Physicians who can confirm the diagnosis and prognosis, and (4) that the patient be competent (Merrell). These obstacles almost eliminate the risks of coercion and manipulation from outside individuals, as well as impulsive and unsure decisions made by the patient.

In the world of healthcare, especially in the practice of PAD, patient autonomy is the most important aspect of medicine. Patient autonomy is the principle that every patient should be able to make their own decisions, independent of influence from family members or healthcare providers. In physician-assisted death, "an autonomy-based approach to assisted suicide regards the provision of assisted suicide (but not euthanasia) as justified when it is autonomously requested by a person, irrespective of whether this is in her best interests" (Braun 497). The ethical justification for this approach is that the patient's reality of long-term and terminal suffering is much more cruel than the reality of a peaceful and dignified death. PAD has also been described as "an expression of the right to a self-determined death," by the German Federal Constitutional Court (Braun 497). This goes off of the basis that every person should have the right to decide whether or not they would like to be alive, which is a decision almost every human possesses. We must pose the question of why this should be any different for terminal patients, depriving them of a dignified and controlled death.

For some terminal patients, simply knowing they have the option of physician-assisted death is a comfort to them, allowing them to feel as though they have control over the end of their lives. A study performed in Canada revealed that within the first 5 years of Medical Aid in dying, the Canadian equivalent of physician-assisted death, 14,405 advanced cancer patients chose to end their lives through assisted dying (Li et al. 3). The study also revealed that 12% of the patients in the study who had a prognosis of less than 6 months presented with a strong and persistent desire for death. While a lot of factors can contribute to a patient's desire to die, one of the biggest contributors is the burden their condition puts on family members/caregivers. The caregivers of these patients must shoulder the task of caring for their loved ones, while also coming to terms with the reality of the terminal conditions. This has a strong impact on mental health of both the caregiver and the patient. The fear of the unavoidable suffering that comes with their diagnosis, combined with the desire to avoid burdening others are considered the strongest reasons why patients choose to utilize MAiD.

Patient advocates for physician-assisted death have spoken up about the hypocrisy of the American Medical Association when it comes to PAD and cancer treatments. Barbara Green, a Virginia resident who was diagnosed with pancreatic cancer, has spoken out about the cruelty of terminal cancer and its treatments versus the practice of PAD. Green said, "They can give me horrible chemotherapy drugs that make me very sick, but they can't give me a drug to help me die peacefully if I'm at that point? I just—I don't understand it" (Paviour). Green brings up a strong point here, reminding us that the treatment of aggressive cancers, specifically pancreatic cancer, is extremely unpleasant and even painful. Giving patients a voice in the matter, which holds some influence, is a crucial part of the public discourse about PAD. Medical professionals can look at the topic from a biological and medical point of view; however, unless either they or a family member has experienced terminal cancer, they cannot provide what is most important in a discussion like this: evidence from personal experience. Some critics claim that instead of having physician-assisted death as an option, medical professionals should focus on "reducing pain and addressing anxiety and depression, not hastening the end of a patient's life" (Paviour). Well, this approach may be effective in certain situations; it gives control of the patient's lives over to their diseases. PAD gives control back to those patients, allowing them to decide when, where, and how their stories end.

In the discussion of physician-assisted death, the main topic is always surrounding the patients, their feelings, and their decisions, and rightfully so considering they are the group the practice affects the most. However, the next group that is affected the most is the families of terminally ill patients. When asked if they would support the legalization and use of PAD, 51% of the family members said that they would support it, 30% would oppose it, and 19% were undecided (Ganzini et al. 232). The leading factors in the decision of whether or not to utilize PAD were levels of religiousness, political views, and concern for personal health. As family members have a strong sense of pain levels, suffering, and quality of life in patients, they are an ideal group to ask for opinions on the matter. Family members are greatly affected by the availability of physician-assisted death. Watching a loved one suffer through cancer treatment is unbearable most of the time, and has extremely strong effects on both the patient and the family. Most of the time, a patient's family does not know where the patient stands on PAD. Discussing the option of physician-assisted death between family members can be upsetting, and even bring up feelings of guilt for all parties involved.

Another crucial party involved in the public discourse of physician-assisted death is the healthcare providers, primarily the nurses. With the involvement of nurses and primary HCPs, we have found that there are five major factors that influence the decisions of patients regarding PAD, including "(1) relationships as central to beginning the process, (2) social and political influences on decision making, (3) complex roles and responsibilities of family members and health-care providers, (4) a unique experience of death, and (5) varying experiences following death" (Variath et al. 1501). As these factors vary from patient to patient, so will their likelihood to value the option of physician-assisted death. Nurses are taught that autonomy is the biggest part of patient care and that they must respect the patient's decision regardless of outside factors or pressures. If a patient knows their nurse is someone whom they may have mutual respect with, they will feel more open to asking questions about physician-assisted care, later aiding in their decision-making process.

The experience of nurses and healthcare providers is crucial to their role in and willingness to provide physician-assisted death. The effects of these experiences are mainly seen within the institutional policies of hospitals and care facilities alike. A nurse's role in the physician-assisted death process is patient support. This entails making sure the patient is comfortable, answering any questions prior to and during the process, and carrying out final requests from the patient (within reason). This process is commonly described by nurses and HCPs as "psychologically and emotionally challenging" (Variath et al. 1502). Building a close relationship with a terminal patient is always difficult, but when PAD is concerned, it can be even more challenging due to how close you must become with not only the patient but the family as well.

When discussing the ethical nature of physician-assisted death, a closer look at the different elements that influence PAD is necessary, from eligibility requirements to familial opinions and healthcare professional experiences is necessary. The concept of patient autonomy comes up as the most prominent pillar, highlighting the critical importance of respecting people's right to make decisions about their own lives, even, and especially, when they are terminally sick. The substantial procedural measures in place attempt to alleviate concerns about coercion and guarantee that PAD remains a voluntary and autonomous decision. These factors make it immensely difficult to come to a verdict on the ethical quality that would be 100% correct, but the majority of the evidence proves that physician-assisted death should be completely legalized and accessible to terminal patients meeting the criteria.

Works Cited

Benedict, S et al. "Historical, Ethical, and Legal Aspects of Assisted Suicide." *The Journal of the Association of Nurses in AIDS Care: JANAC,* vol. 9, no. 2, 1998, pp. 34–44. doi:10.1016/S1055-3290(98)80059-9.

Braun, Esther. "An Autonomy-Based Approach to Assisted Suicide: A Way to Avoid the Expressivist Objection Against Assisted Dying Laws." *Journal of Medical Ethics,* vol. 49, no. 7, 2023, pp. 497–501. doi:10.1136/jme-2022-108375.

Ganzini, Linda, et al. "Views on Physician-Assisted Suicide Among Family Members of Oregon Cancer Patients." *Journal of Pain and Symptom Management,* vol. 32, no. 3, Sept. 2006, pp. 230–36, https://doi.org/10.1016/j.jpainsymman.2006.04.004.

Lee, Myung Ah. "Ethical Issue of Physician-Assisted Suicide and Euthanasia." *Journal of Hospice and Palliative Care,* vol. 26, no. 2, Korean Society for Hospice and Palliative Care, June 2023, pp. 95–100, https://doi.org10.14475/jhpc.2023.26.2.95.

Li, Madeline, et al. "Medical Assistance in Dying in Patients with Advanced Cancer and Their Caregivers: A Mixed Methods Longitudinal Study Protocol." *BMC Palliative Care,* vol. 20, no. 1, Springer Science and Business Media LLC, July 2021, p. 117, https://doi.org10.1186/s12904-021-00793-4.

Merrell., Don A. "How Not to Think About the Autonomy-Based Argument for Physician-Assisted Suicide." *Psychiatric Times,* 22 Feb. 2023, www.psychiatrictimes.com/view/how-not-to-think-about-the-autonomy-based-argument-for-physician-assisted-suicide.

National Academies of Sciences, Engineering, and Medicine, et al. "Conceptual, Legal, and Ethical Considerations in Physician-Assisted Death." *National Academies Press,* 2017, https://www.ncbi.nlm.nih.gov/books/NBK525943/.

Paviour, Ben. "Virginia Lawmakers Consider Proposal to Legalize Physician-Assisted Death." *NPR,* 8 Feb. 2024, www.npr.org/2024/02/08/1229935048/virginia-lawmakers-consider-proposal-to-legalize-physician-assisted-death.

Variath, Caroline, et al. "Relational Influences on Experiences with Assisted Dying: A Scoping Review." *Nursing Ethics,* vol. 27, no. 7, SAGE Publications, Nov. 2020, pp. 1501–1516, https://doi.org10.1177/.

Questions to Consider

1. Summer chose a controversial and often emotionally-loaded subject to research and approached her process from a neutral or inquiry-based perspective. What are the benefits of beginning a research process with an open mind, from an inquiry-based perspective? How might that look different from choosing a topic on which you already have a strong opinion? How do you think this attitude affects the tone or outcome of a finished research-based argument?

2. Summer advised students to take what they learn from the Rhetorical Analysis paper and apply it to their own writing. What rhetorical appeals do you see at work in this essay? Which appeals do you find the strongest or most convincing? How might you learn from her application of rhetorical strategies and apply it to your own arguments?

3. This essay begins with a hypothetical story about a person who is suffering from a terminal illness and chooses Physician-Assisted Death before moving into the next paragraph, which offers an overview of the issue under examination and ends in a thesis statement. What rhetorical work does the narrative opening provide? Why might Summer have chosen to open with a story rather than an overview of the issue? How does this strategy affect or connect with an audience differently than a less personal approach?

Troubled Teens or Teens in Trouble? An In-Depth Analysis of The Troubled Teen Industry and its Effects

Bryn Powers
Honorable Mention for Research-Based Argument

Reflection

I found out the truth about the Troubled Teen Industry a couple years ago through a web article and in true ADHD fashion, went down a rabbit hole of stories, testimonies, and protests of the industry. When picking a topic for this paper, I knew I wanted to do something semi-controversial, and that few people would know about. I remembered my internet deep dive and decided to research and share my knowledge of the abusive industry.

Some advice I would offer first year writers for this assignment is to pick a topic you're passionate about because it makes the process of researching, writing, and revising so much more enjoyable. When you're researching a topic that really interests you, it barely feels like work and makes it easier to write something you're proud of.

Content Warning

This essay contains discussions of sexual assault, physical, and emotional abuse.

Troubled Teens or Teens in Trouble? An In-Depth Analysis of The Troubled Teen Industry and its Effects

What do you do when your teen is acting out? Therapy? Communication? Your answer should be anything but sending them to a wilderness therapy camp or residential treatment facility, both parts of the troubled teen industry. The troubled teen industry is the system of highly unregulated residential youth treatment facilities operating primarily in the United States. Adolescents are sent to these programs for a variety of reasons including by their parents for behavioral issues, and by juvenile court order. It's not uncommon for programs like these to be inhumane, abusive, and traumatic. Many people believe the troubled teen industry and wilderness therapy to be beneficial for adolescents struggling behaviorally at home or in school, but I am going to show you why it's actually quite harmful for the victims of the industry. The troubled teen industry creates poor parent-child relationships, negatively affects mental health of adolescents, is not proven to be beneficial, and has killed thousands of children and teenagers across the United States.

The troubled teen industry has been around for roughly 60 years according to C. Jamie Mater in her article "The Troubled Teen Industry and its Effects." An uncountable number of children and adolescents are put into troubled teen programs across the country every year and thousands remain in them today. These programs are highly unregulated and therefore get away with a lot of shady practices such as starvation, overworking, and in extreme cases, abuse. Kids are sometimes sent to troubled teen programs by juvenile justice court or by their school, but it is often the child's own parents who blindly spend hundreds to send their kids to these programs because they don't know what else to do with their misbehaving child. Lack of accurate information provided about the programs convinces parents that the therapy will change their lives and magically heal their child when in reality there is no proof that any of the methods practiced in these types of programs actually works. The industry is comprised of a variety of programs including wilderness therapy programs, residential treatment facilities, therapeutic boarding schools and more, all falling under the umbrella of the Troubled Teen Industry.

Many treatment facilities create a rift between children and their parents. Misleading advertising about wilderness therapy programs such as promising a changed child once treatment is over, when in reality the therapy provided causes the exact opposite effect. Parents who don't know what to do with their kids when they act out opt to send their children to residential facilities blindly, without knowing the full extent of what occurs within them. In his article "When I was Labeled a 'Troubled' Teen, I Obliged," Kenneth Rosen explains how going to a wilderness therapy program ruined his relationship with his parents, and why the program was so harmful for his physical and mental wellbeing. He writes, "My parents were no longer trustworthy. They were part of the growing number of my adversaries working to keep me from personal liberties. At the program I was restricted access to food. I was allowed only communication with my parents, not my friends back home" (Rosen). This quote gives us not only an example of the emotional strain put on his relationship with his parents, but also provides a glimpse into the mistreatment Rosen endured while he was a participant of the program.

Within the many accounts of troubled teen industry survivors, food restriction and limited contact with the outside world were two common ways staff at residential programs would gain control over the young people in their "care." Rosen mentions in his article how he was only allowed to send letters to his parents about how he was doing, no one else. He also explains how if he were to refuse to send the letters to his parents, he would be cut off from his peers in the program, making it a lose-lose either way (Rosen). Many survivors of the troubled teen industry also report being abused physically and, in some instances, sexually. Activist and author Liz Ianelli shares her story with the *New York Times* as well, "she said her 'therapy' for most of the next three years consisted of daily emotional attacks by staff and fellow students, forced labor, food deprivation and other assaults. While there, she was also raped by a kitchen employee, she reports. Then, as punishment for 'lying' about it, she was bound in a blanket with duct tape and left in a boiler room for eight days" (Szalavitz). Abuse and neglect such as this seem to be a common occurrence within facilities like the one Liz was a victim of. Starvation and abuse not only affect a child physically, but also take a toll on their mental wellbeing.

Many wilderness therapy programs have also been shown to negatively affect their participants mental health and cause lasting damage. From kidnapping kids out of their beds in the middle of the night, to physically abusing them, to using inhumane punishments to keep kids' behavior in line, these young, impressionable minds are severely and irreversibly damaged from the treatment within wilderness therapy. Depression and anxiety are common and sometimes amplified due to the conditions. In her article, "The Troubled Teen Industry and its Effects," C. Jamie Mater spoke to many victims of the troubled teen industry and found that participants commonly felt anxious, hopeless, and trapped while in the programs. "One participant recalled, 'I was always on edge, thinking, what am I doing wrong right now?' Another 'felt empty, like an experiment or a puppet.' Overall, participants' 'emotional needs weren't being met.' Most coped with difficult times by dissociating, because 'it was better than feeling the reality of being there'" (Mater 6). From these accounts, it can be gathered that the participants often weren't benefiting from their treatment but actually being hurt instead. It is not uncommon for the teens sent to facilities such as these to already suffer from mental health issues, so the stress and anxiety the programs induce cause the kids more harm than good.

The effects of residential programs go beyond mental health issues within the camp. PTSD is common among survivors of wilderness therapy. Through research done by Mater, they explain how experiences within these programs can cause lasting trauma that survivors can carry with them to this day. Being reintroduced into society was difficult on its own, without considering the participants commonly experiencing nightmares, panic attacks, and memory issues. Mater says, "Some participants struggled soon after their release, while others experienced a brief period of believing they were mentally healthy, followed by a crash. Several were admitted to mental hospitals within a year" (Mater 7). This prevalent occurrence of a "mental crash" proves that the wilderness programs these troubled teens were being sent to weren't actually helping them, but simply traumatizing them and at the very most providing a temporary fix to a deeper issue. For teens with drug addiction issues, relapsing is common once released, and others developed eating disorders due to the deprivation of food they experience while in the programs.

Mental health isn't the only damage wilderness therapy programs cause, however. Countless deaths have been recorded at the hands of residential facilities; from starvation to suicides, the list is endless. A blog made by Danes includes an incomplete list of the deaths, which are organized by program, age, and cause of death, dating all the way back to 1971. Common causes of death include restraint, drowning, starvation and several cases of participants found hanging or other ways of suicide. This list becomes even more devastating when learning the average age of the victims was 14. The youngest life taken on the blog's list was 7-year-old Angellika Arndt, from restraint. Angellika died at Northwest Counseling and Guidance Clinic Rice Lake. A location that has since been shut down, but the company still remains operational with several locations across rural Wisconsin. Angellika was allegedly restrained nine times and put in time out eighteen times during her stay at the program (WebWire). The Department of Health and Family Services reports that each restraint of Arndt lasted 1–2 hours and the final restraint caused her to lose consciousness and never regain it (WebWire). Denison Tucker, the president of this program, claimed that his staff were trained and licensed, but if the hold was executed correctly, Angellika may still be alive.

Many participants also experience physical abuse and a large portion of the active programs in the US have sexual assault allegations. An example of this institutional abuse is the Provo Canyon School which happens to be the location that American media personality Paris Hilton was sent when she was a teenager. Eight former participants spoke of their experiences and the treatment they witnessed while students at Provo Canyon School. They described physical restraints, overmedication, chemical sedation, and isolation rooms as methods used to gain control over the students. Despite these condemnations, Provo Canyon is still open and has remained this way for over 50 years (Miller). This is a familiar story for many former participants, as countless residential facilities have several conduct and/or assault allegations and remain open despite them. Unfortunately, many of the staff at residential programs haven't undergone the proper training and don't know how to deal with kids when they act out.

Despite how dismal the troubled teen industry may seem, there is some good being done to advocate for those negatively affected by the system. According to a press release by Wagstaff and Cartmell Law Firm, partner Diane K. Watkins has taken on the role of fighting for the rights of the victims affected by and currently within the industry. Watkins says she wants to be a voice for the voiceless, seeking justice for those who have endured maltreatment at the hands of this industry (qtd. in Wagstaff and Cartmell). Watkins is not only helping those affected by the troubled teen industry but is also helping raise awareness. Internet personality Paris Hilton has also spoken up about being a survivor of the industry. Having a person like Hilton speak out about her experiences and talk about ways we can help other victims is hugely beneficial for finding solutions. The majority of people have no idea what goes on at these facilities which is why it's so important to raise awareness and begin to make change happen. Hilton acknowledges and supports the work of lawyers like Watkins for doing this kind of work, saying, "Their commitment to justice and willingness to fight for those who have been silenced is not just admirable, it's essential. Together, we can make a real difference and ensure that the voices of survivors are not just heard, but are catalysts for change" (qtd. in Wagstaff and Cartmell). The power of celebrities and other people in the public eye speaking out against social issues such as this is immeasurable, which is also why it's so important Hilton talks about her experience.

It is estimated that 100,000 kids are held in residential facilities annually, but that number can't be verified because of how unregulated they are. The unregulated nature of these facilities is exactly why they're so dangerous. There are no rules about how the programs are allowed to punish their participants, and there's not even any proof that this kind of treatment is actually effective. The fact that not many people know the truth about this industry is a huge problem. Spreading awareness about the troubled teen industry and beginning to boycott and protest the programs within it is the first step to ridding the world of the industry completely.

Works Cited

"About Northwest Counseling and Guidance Clinic." *NWCGC,* 2023, nwcgc.com/about/.

Danes. "Victims of the Troubled Teen Industry in the United States." *1000 Places You Don't Want to Be as a Teenager,* 8 Feb. 2024, 1000placesudontwanttobe.wordpress.com/victims-of-the-troubled-teen-industry/.

Miller, Jessica. "After a Riot, Increasing Violence and Now Sex Abuse Allegations, Red Rock Canyon School Will Close." *The Salt Lake Tribune,* 10 July 2019, www.sltrib.com/news/2019/07/10/after-riot-increasing/.

Miller, Jessica. "Provo Canyon School's History of Abuse Accusations Spans Decades, Far beyond Paris Hilton." *The Salt Lake Tribune,* 20 Sept. 2020, www.sltrib.com/news/2020/09/20/provo-canyon-schools/.

Okoren, Nicolle. "The Wilderness 'Therapy' That Teens Say Feels like Abuse: 'You Are on Guard at All Times.'" *The Guardian, Guardian News and Media,* 14 Nov. 2022, www.theguardian.com/us-news/2022/nov/14/us-wilderness-therapy-camps-troubled-teen-industry-abuse.

Rosen, Kenneth R. "When I Was Labeled a 'Troubled' Teen, I Obliged." *The New York Times,* The New York Times, 12 Jan. 2021, www.nytimes.com/2021/01/12/well/family/teen-tough-love-programs.html.

Salt Lake Tribune. "Read the Violation Reports and Inspections for Utah's 'Troubled-Teen' Treatment Centers." *The Salt Lake Tribune,* 4 Mar. 2021, www.sltrib.com/footer/2021/03/04/read-violation-reports/.

Szalavitz, Maia. "The Troubled-Teen Industry Offers Trauma, Not Therapy." *The New York Times,* The New York Times, 19 Oct. 2023, www.nytimes.com/2023/10/19/opinion/troubled-teens-industry-regulation.html.

"Wagstaff & Cartmell Partner Diane K. Watkins Becomes Advocate for Victims in the Troubled Teen Industry; Recognized by Paris Hilton." *Plus Company Updates,* 10 Feb. 2024, p. NA. *Gale OneFile: Business,* link.gale.com/apps/doc/A782868898/ITBC?u=xavier_main&sid=ebsco&xid=497614c3. Accessed 21 Feb. 2024.

Zehnder, Isabelle. "Death of 7-Year Old Angellika Arndt Results in Closure of Northwest's Rice Lake Clinic." *WebWire,* WEBWIRE, 2 Aug. 2006, www.webwire.com/ViewPressRel.asp?aId=17798.

Questions to Consider

1. Bryn chose a subject that is not well-known or talked about a lot but had caught her interest. What are the goals and purpose of this essay? Why might it be important to bring lesser-known issues to light through research and writing? What should readers do, think, or believe if Bryn's rhetorical appeals are successful?

2. Many of the sources Bryn uses in this essay are from popular press and journalistic articles. Why might this topic call for the use of popular sources? In what contexts might it be necessary or more effective to examine newspapers as sources for an argument? How does Bryn use the information from these sources and integrate it with her own ideas?

3. This essay deals with abuse to minors, who have found themselves in terrible situations with very little power. What does it add to the argument to hear quotes from victims of these abuses speaking about their experiences? How do the stories of real people add to the overall rhetorical effectiveness of this essay? What rhetorical appeals are at work in the sources and quotes that Bryn has utilized in this argument?

The Need for All Books in School

Gillian Ocampo
Honorable Mention for Research-Based Argument

Reflection

At the start of the semester, we were all asked to pick a controversial topic to focus on for our writing pieces. Looking at the list, all the popular topics were listed like abortion, gun control, and animal captivity; however, one topic stood out to me: book banning. While many people may view this as a "boring" topic, I found that it related to all the other topics on the list. Books give us the chance to imagine walking in someone else's shoes, to learn about something we knew nothing about before, and to hear the stories of people we have never met. In 7th grade my class read *Fahrenheit 451,* a dystopian novel which followed a firefighter whose job was not to put out fires but instead start them. He was tasked with burning any and all books found. In my high school U.S. history class, I learned about the censorship in Nazi Germany and the Confederacies attempts to ban *Uncle Tom's Cabin,* which can be credited to swinging the outcome of the Civil War in the Union's favor. These powerful stories of books' influence in history and the possible future compelled me to investigate the issue in light of today's politics.

When writing my piece, I often found it challenging to find articles covering the topic that did more than just bash the opposing side. It was hard to find pieces that gave deeper reasoning for their opinions. However, once I cracked the surface, I found a world of research which not only looked at the immediate psychological effects on students faced with books bans, but also on the long-term effects on the community and students' physical health in relation to bullying. In my revision process I found it helpful to have my peers in my class read over my draft and add comments. We were all in the same boat with the same assignment but each a different topic. I found their feedback to be the most helpful because they understood my struggles to word something just right or to convey my proposal. I never went to the Writing Center but my friends who did said it was super helpful for getting a fresh set of eyes on a paper or to help jumpstart an outline. I would also recommend getting a fresh set of eyes to read over your paper. I asked a friend who had not even taken the class, and she gave me great feedback because she read it with no background information on the topic or prompt. Her feedback was super objective and helped me identify areas where my writing may be clear to me or my classmates, but not so much someone less familiar with the assignment.

The Need for All Books in School

In 1922, a man's pride and joy were ripped from circulation due to a judge's opinion that it was "the work of a disordered mind." This book was banned for over a decade, losing the author unknown amounts in royalties as well as the right to see his work on shelves (Brady). Why are people so afraid of their children reading the stories of minority individuals that these stories must be wiped from the shelves of school libraries and placed behind lock and key? Books provide diverse perspectives, opportunities to learn from mistakes and freedom of speech; therefore, local and state governments should not be able to ban books due to the negative effects on society as well as the violation of citizens first amendment rights. By prohibiting bans but facilitating discussions and support within the classroom, schools can help guide and support students in dealing with these difficult topics. This approach opens schools to safe learning environments where students can freely talk about these challenging subjects.

The History of Book Banning in America

Book banning has come and gone throughout history, ranging in extent and classification. In the United States, the first book that was banned on a national scale was Harriet Beecher Stowe's *Uncle Tom's Cabin*. The book featured pro-abolitionist views and stirred the debate regarding slavery which caused it to be banned by the Confederacy prior to the Civil War (Brady). The next major ban in the U.S. was several years after the war when Congress signed into effect a law prohibiting the mailing of what they deemed "pornographic material." The definition was loose and encompassed anything from anatomy textbooks to *The Canterbury Tales* (Brady). The 1920s saw a shift toward free reader movements which advocated for citizens' right to read whatever they wanted. The next major event was the case of *The United States v. One Book Called Ulysses* in which the 1922 banning of the book, *Ulysses,* was overturned by Judge John M. Woolsey on the basis that "sex, even if unpleasant, should be allowed in serious literature." In 1957, a second layer to the ruling was made in which the courts ruled that the ban on the mailing of pornographic materials only applied to those which are "utterly without redeeming social importance." Woosley had deemed *Ulysses* to carry some social importance and therefore undeserving of a ban (Brady). This case set the precedent for bans today and is often used in resistance to bans arguing that every book has social importance because they each convey a unique perspective valuable in itself.

Much of the history of book banning in America is intertwined with the citizens' Constitutional First Amendment rights. This led to the rise of Banned Books Week in 1982 by the ALA which prompted the freedom to read and inform readers of the issue by advertising banned or challenged books. Many people may not be aware that their favorite books or those they consider classics are at the forefront of the heated debate. Well known titles such as *Fahrenheit 451, The Giving Tree,* and *To Kill a Mockingbird,* which are often taught in schools and commonly referenced, are some of these such books. These books have been taught in school for decades and many students, such as myself, have read and analyzed them in classroom settings. While *To Kill a Mockingbird* has racial content, within the classroom we identified terms which are derogatory and social norms that marginalize and harm the characters of color. These guided discussions created an environment for reflection and according to the article, "Key Lessons from Book Bannings," over 2,000 books have been challenged or removed from schools and libraries across the

US (Liou and Cutler). Thousands of books each year are removed from schools. While they are still available in bookstores and public libraries, children must read them on their own as they are prohibited in schools, which should be places for discussion.

The Need for Diverse Perspectives in Books

One of the most important reasons books should not be banned is because they offer a window into a world of diverse perspectives. In her article "Harmful to Minors" Pickering notes that "in the first six months of the academic year 2022–23, 30% of the unique titles were books about race, racism, or those with characters of color. Twenty-six percent featured LGBTQ+ protagonists or stories." Children who relate to these characters may feel alone or unheard if these books are removed from schools. Other students will also lose the opportunity to empathize with others and miss hearing their stories if such books are removed. David, a high school student from Muskegon, Michigan, writes in a currents events conversation that through reading books featuring other gay characters he was reassured he was not alone. He also writes that attempts to remove LGBTQIA+ contents from schools is straight up hurtful because it makes him feel alone and targeted (Nguyen). These stories give him something to relate and empathize with. The removal of such books not only takes away this connection but it also makes him and others like him question if it is not just the books the schools are hoping to silence but also the individuals like him. These negative thoughts can lead to feelings of isolation, as a parent and the cofounder of the Florida Freedom to Read Project, Staphanie Ferrell, emphasizes the possible psychological impact book banning may have on students, such as the feeling "targeted and devalued through explicit and implicit messages that books affirming their histories and lived experiences do not have any academic values" (Pickering).

Those in Favor of Book Bans

Some people believe that "book bans" are necessary in school settings to protect the young and innocent minds of children. They argue that certain books that contain inappropriate or graphic material such as rape, violence, and racial prejudices should not be available in schools because they may be harmful to students. In "Florida at Center of Debate as School Book Bans Surge Nationally," Jennifer Pippin, a leader of a local chapter of Moms for Liberty in Florida voices her concern that children may, "happen to pick up a book that contains a graphic rape scene … because they enjoyed others volumes in the same series" (Alter et al.). Schools should be safe learning environments and parents should have control over what their students have access to. They also argue for the removal of books which include racist language because it is not appropriate for students in this age. For instance, a school district in Washington removed *To Kill a Mockingbird* from their curriculum because of its use of racist language and depictions of race relations (Zurcher). Parents not only want to protect their children from the violence or rape but also the emotional harm that racist texts can evoke. The authors of the article argue that books which have been removed from school libraries in certain states should "not be considered 'banned' because they remain audible at public libraries and in bookstores" (Alter et al.). They argue for the removal of certain books merely from the school libraries where teachers and administrators are held responsible for student activities.

Response to Those in Favor of Book Bans

The opposition make a fine point that books removed from schools are not, in the entirety of the word, "banned." However, their argument for protecting students' minds and that schools are a safe learning environment seems like it would suggest that schools are the best place for such books since they offer students the most support to decipher such texts. Intellectually, experts advise against students reading heavy material on their own; "instead, they advocate for parents, librarians, educators, and other adults to go through the material with the student. To talk to them about the issues that arise from a book" (Pickering). With proper support systems in place, students can gain a diverse understanding of the lived experiences and history of historically marginalized groups while at the same time having support and guidance to deal with these difficult topics. These are important topics that are part of everyday life and which students will most likely encounter. Schools should be safe learning environments which should be used to regulate and facilitate discussion around these topics so that students have the support and guidance needed to foster mature conversations. To add to that, banned books are not as dangerous to students as some parents fear. In "Key Lessons from Book Bannings," a case study investigated these relationships and found that diverse books and anti-racist curriculum saw increased graduation rates and aided students' ability to interpret racist bullying contributing to improved school safety (Liou and Cutler). By providing voices to the oppressed, books promote empathy, foster connections between people, and promote conversation and community.

In 1984, Evelyn Feller reminded the world that "censorship emblematizes the classic liberal dilemma: the responsibility of a democracy to allow free expression to the most repugnant of idea, even those that deny the very principles of freedom on which that hospitality is based" (Kidd 200). This undermines many of supporters of the bans arguments, because no matter the opinion of the book, whether liberal, conservative, racist, or woke, each book has a story to share which is protected under the First Amendment. In the case, *Board of Education v. Pico,* the court held that the removal of books from schools violates the Constitution depending on "the motivation behind the removal. If an official intends to deny children access to ideas with which they disagree, and this intent is the 'decisive factor' in the ban, the ban is unconstitutional" (Beavers 12). This case declares that the removal of books based on the undesirable ideas which they share is unconstitutional. The opponent's argument of the perceived harmful impact on students does not meet the requirements for banning and is therefore an infringement upon the rights protected unto the Constitution. All voices have a right to be heard and infringement upon this right directly attacks the very foundation this nation is built on.

Qualifying the Cry to Prohibit Book Bans

Sophomore English major, Aubrey Jackson, argues in her opinion article "Approach with Caution: Some Books are Banned for a Reason" that while no books should be banned, some should not be promoted. She specifically focuses on Jay Ashers, *13 Reasons Why,* which depicts scenes of rape, suicide, depression, and gun violence. Jackson includes that the author, Asher, regularly receives praise from fans of the book and 2017 Netflix film on how it "made them feel seen or even prompted them to get help." However, Jackson notes the "notoriety for [it] being a triggering and largely inaccurate portrayal of teenage depression and suicide" and a study by Carnegie Mellon University found that, "in the months immediately following the release of the show, the suicide rate for teens aged 10 to 17 years increased significantly" (Aubrey). Aubrey identifies an important distinction to make between banned books and books worth reading. While she believes books should be available to everyone, not all books should be promoted to children simply because they address social issues. It is still important to be able to make the distinction between the stories of real people and the generalized and often erroneous representations of groups no matter what side of society or history they identify with. Books share these stories and bans take away the opportunity to share these stories.

Solution

In the end, books should not be banned. Schools are meant to be safe learning environments and we should talk about the content of the books, their flaws, and drawbacks, but not ban them. Keeping all books in schools without talking about them can make the fears of parents come true. Some historic books have unjust portrayals of certain groups or language not appropriate today; however, kids should understand and be able to identify this so that they understand it is not okay. Simply banning books infringes on rights and will lead to upset or dumb and easily controlled society through government overreach. This is seen in one of the challenged books, *Fahrenheit 451,* where books were burned and citizens banned from reading (Nguyen). Additionally, statistics show the benefits to students when they are exposed to diverse perspectives in books. It is important to recognize the history of book banning in the US and learn from their mistakes. Through investigating this history, it has become clear that many arguments to support the banning of books are unconstitutional and go directly against past precedents. By recognizing the good in books and the negative effects of bans, we can move forward and welcome the ever diverse world we live in and grow to understand and respect the unique stories of every individual. Students can find allies in books, people to relate or look up to, as well as lessons to learn from and to develop empathy for others. This will be a gateway to mature conversation between students, teachers, parents, and neighbors.

Works Cited

Beavers, Anna. "Balancing Interests: Harmful Bans & Harmful Books." *2 We the People,* Elon L. Const. L.J. 1, 23 May 2023, SSRN: https://ssrn.com/abstract=4717160.

Bradley, Amy. "The History (and Present) of Banning Books in America." *Literary Hub,* 2 Apr. 2021, lithub.com/the-history-and-present-of-banning-books-in-america.

ChatGPT. "Give me a solution to book banning that protects authors freedom of speak and minority voices while also protecting minors" prompt. ChatGPT, GPT-4, OpenAI, DATE, chat.openai.com/chat.

Cutler, Kelly Deits and Daniel D. Liou. "Key Lessons from Book Bans: Critical Literacy as a Practice of Freedom." *Literacy Today (2411–7862),* vol. 41, no. 1, July 2023, pp. 44–49.

Jackson, Aubrey. "Approach with Caution: Some Books are Banned for a Reason." *Trinitonian,* 13 October 2023, Approach with caution: Some books are banned for a reason—Trinitonian.

Kidd, Kenneth. "'Not Censorship but Selection': Censorship and/as Prizing." *Children's Literature in Education* 40:197–216, 2 December 2008, DOI 10.1007/s10583-008-9078-4.

Nguyen, Viet Thanh. "My Young Mind Was Disturbed by a Book. It Changed My Life." *The New York Times,* The New York Times, 29 Jan. 2022, www.nytimes.com/2022/01/29/opinion/culture/book-banning-viet-thanh-nguyen.html.

Pickering, Grace. "'Harmful to Minors': How Book Bans Hurt Adolescent Development." *Serials Librarian,* vol. 84, no. 1–4, Jan. 2023, pp. 32–45. https://doi.org/10.1080/0361526X.2023.2245843.

Zurcher, Anthony. "Why are Certain School Books Being Banned in US?" *BBC news,* 7 February 2022, Why are certain school books being banned in US? (bbc.com).

Questions to Consider

1. One of the distinctive features of this essay is the way that it is organized around sub-headings that announce which part of the argument is coming up in that section. As a reader, how did this affect your ability to follow or understand the argument? If headings hadn't been an option, what other ways could the writer have indicated the parts of the argument that were coming next? What effect do the headings have upon the rhetorical effectiveness of the essay overall?

2. Gillian presents multiple sides of this issue, making her own position clear, but also including and responding to other positions. How does this affect her ethos as a writer? Does it add to, or detract from, her argument to include other opinions on this issue? What is the purpose of including counter-arguments and rebuttals of those positions within an argument?

3. In the Works Cited, Gillian appropriately credits ChatGPT for helping her come up with a solution to a difficult problem with multiple sides. Can you imagine other solutions that might satisfy the same criteria? What other positions can you think of for the controversy surrounding book banning? Are there other positions that might not be included in this particular essay? What might they be and how would you address them?

Institutionalized Racism — A Call for Change

Destiny Starks
Honorable Mention for Research-Based Argument

Reflection

This paper was a challenge that I may have inflicted on
myself. A big challenge came with organizing all the ideas in a way that flew
and made sense. In creating my outline, I had a lot of different points that I
could touch on, which was a great thing as I would rather have too much than
too little. While I did not plan on talking about each point, my challenge was
deciding which points were worth discussing even though they all felt equally
important. Finding time to work on a paper so lengthy also came as a challenge
for me with my major. However, creating different talking points went well for
me. I was able to fill in the outline blueprint without much of a problem as I
already had some ideas of the things I wanted to discuss. With that completed,
finding sources to support my different talking points went well.

There are a lot of articles surrounding this controversy which made the process much easier. However, finding a counterargument came as a challenge
because there are not many sources that talk about racism being a good thing. I
believe we used AI (Chat GPT) to give us possible solutions for our controversy,
which did not come as a challenge to me. I had my draft peer reviewed and I
made revisions by incorporating more ethos into my paper. I also made sure to
properly integrate quotations into my body paragraphs in ways that made sense
to readers and gave greater clarity and understanding. I decided to talk about
this topic because it is something very close and personal to me. It is something
that I must think about and deal with every day of my life. I would advise
everyone to pick a topic that they are passionate about because it makes it that
much easier to research, understand, learn, and argue your topic.

Institutionalized Racism—A Call for Change

Imagine a world where anybody could truly grow up and become anything that
they wanted to be no matter where they came from, what their hair looked like,
or the color of their skin. While this life may be a reality for some, it is not for
all. Unfortunately, people of color are denied proper housing, jobs, and even
income simply because they are Black. What makes something like this possible? Institutionalized racism. Institutionalized racism, sometimes called systemic racism, is a set of policies and legislation that directly or indirectly benefit
whites and disadvantage colored people. These laws may or may not have
been made with the intention of harming minorities, but nevertheless, they do
when in effect. Because institutionalized racism creates inequality among its
people and negatively affects the mental, emotional, and physical well-being of
colored communities, institutionalized racism needs to be dismembered with
reformed policies, better political representation, and public awareness and
education on the topic.

It is safe to say that this racial discrimination began at the early stages of the establishment of the United States with slavery. During this time in the country, Africans were taken from their homelands, shipped across the Atlantic Ocean, and violently forced into lives of labor, abuse, and captivity. They were viewed as less than human without rights and dignity and were treated accordingly, as revenue. These types of conditions occurred because of the laws in place that allowed for this treatment of humans for over 200 years. There would come a point when the groups of people who did not agree with these unfair conditions would fight against it. The biggest evidence of this rebellion would mark the start of the American Civil War which lasted for about 4 years. The end of slavery came in 1865 with the implementation of legislation that officially banned it. Slaves were released from bondage and ownership; however, they still were not given equal lives and rights as white Americans.

Years after slavery, Black people still suffered from aggression, unfair treatment, and violence from whites in public spaces and government systems. Black people were given physical freedom but still had to deal with inferior treatment, especially with the enforcement of Jim Crow laws. Jim Crow laws allowed for the segregation of Blacks from whites in many public areas such as bathrooms, water fountains, education systems, and neighborhoods. For years many violent acts including lynching and police brutality would go overlooked and unchecked under these laws. Examples include the horrific lynching of 14-year-old Emmett Till who was kidnapped, tortured, and killed by a group of white men. The Black Panther Party, a Black political organization for Black rights, would be established to combat the preexisting and rising police brutality.

While Jim Crow would end, Black people would still be the target of police brutality as the years continued. The lives of Oscar Grant, a Black man who was unnecessarily shot and killed by a cop on New Year's Day, and Rodney King, a Black man who was brutally beaten to death by multiple cops in public, would succumb to police brutality. However, the sudden murder of Trayvon Martin, an African American young man who was wrongfully shot by police, would cause an uproar in the Black community starting the Black Lives Matter Movement after his killers were not convicted of his murder. The Black community continues to deal with the deaths of its members at the hands of white Americans with Elaine Arkin stating, "[P]olice violence is a leading cause of death for young Black men in the United States," instilling a fear and anger within the community (174). This is a powerful statistic because it shows just how much harm and violence is being inflicted on people of color to the point that these violent interactions, not disease or natural circumstances, are the main causes of death in the Black community.

Furthermore, historically over time, there have been different laws that have caused a lot of controversy in the Black community. Controversy exists around laws that have been created to harm people of color in history. The biggest example of this was the implementation of former President Franklin D. Roosevelt's legislation known as The New Deal. According to *The Washington Post*, "To secure the votes needed to pass the bill, Roosevelt agreed to certain exemptions for farmworkers, domestic workers and others that led to generational financial injury for Black and Brown people" (Davidson). This goes to show how historically respected and currently enforced legislation was created without the benefit of people of color in mind; in fact, they were created to disadvantage people of color. These types of laws that ensure the loss of minorities are spread throughout the country's constitution.

Legislation has also become a problem more recently with the Supreme Court passing laws that will dismantle laws that help marginalized communities. The 1965 Voting Rights Act was a big push forward for communities of color as it made the government monitor racial discrimination among voters and render voting discrimination illegal by enforcing the 15th Amendment. According to *The New York Times,* the Supreme Court has not only been overlooking laws that discriminate against people of color in Arizona, but it has voted to keep "laws despite lower federal courts finding clear evidence that the laws make voting harder for voters of color—whether Black, Latino or Native American" ("The Court Abandons Voting Rights"). These recent events within the Supreme Court show that governmental representation has been ignoring clear racial inequalities and implementing more with each law passed.

Institutionalized racism creates many different inequalities in important organizations that negatively impact people of color, including professionally, legally, and residentially. Structural racism has paved the way for inequality in the workplace by allowing the creation and termination of jobs based on race. In fact, a school director shared their experience stating, "I've seen great teachers fired because they were Black and I've seen people treated awful because they were Black" (Brooks 646). This personal testimony shows how racism is presented in professional workspaces and how it is perceived by others. It also demonstrates the negative effect professional inequity has on others simply because of their skin color. The creation of these discriminatory workspaces is allowed and influenced by different government regulations, setting the colored people back in the workforce community.

Systemic racism has been shown to create living inequalities between different races. Segregation has now been implemented in the form of housing communities of marginalized citizens in populated areas with little resources. These areas have become so common that they have been given a name, the ghettos. These trends have been noticed by many with some even finding that "African American and Latino people are more likely than White people with similar household incomes to live in neighborhoods with concentrated disadvantages" (Arkin et al. 173). This research shows how people of color are disproportionately impacted by not being given the same opportunities as white Americans even though their incomes are equal. Some disadvantages, according to Arkin et al., "include well-documented patterns of selectively locating coal-fired power plants and hazardous waste disposal in or near communities of color" (173). Arkin et al. shows how dangerous and life-threatening the conditions people of color are left to populate. Legislation affects the housing of colored communities as it allows home and landowners to have biases when choosing tenants. This racial discrimination forces people of color to choose options that are unsuitable, unsafe, and under-resourced because that is all they can afford or that will accept them.

Moreover, there have been effects on the criminalization of Black people. It is no secret that the colored community and the police force have had a rocky relationship. However, the factual evidence of these inequalities in the criminal justice system continues to grow with time. Black people are put in jail at higher rates and given longer sentences on average compared to their white counterparts. Statistics show that "Black people were admitted at four times the rate of white people on an average in 2022" ("Racial Disparities Persist in Many U.S. Jails"). This illustrates that the minorities of the population are being imprisoned at rates and quantities much higher than that of the majority, making them the majority in crime, which goes against most logical reasoning as one would expect the majority to remain in its position in its community. These gaps are made possible by the laws that govern the prison system and are heavily influenced by the overcriminalization of Black people. This overcriminalization begins at a young age in the education system. The issue, today known as the school-to-prison pipeline, is explained by Arkin et al. as "children … of color [being] systemically disciplined more harshly than other children for behavioral problems" (174). Arkin's definition goes to show that Black students are treated differently in government institutions in their youth which in turn predisposes them to further discrimination in the justice system in their lifetime. This evidence negatively impacts people of color by taking away their freedom and impacting their abilities to obtain necessary resources for life, such as housing and jobs, following their incarceration.

In addition, racial disparities affect the mental and emotional well-being of Black people. As systemic racism continues to grow, so do the emotions of its affected people. After being treated a bad way for so long, negative feelings begin to develop in association. Jeffery Brooks writes the testimony of an African American school manager stating, "Racism is real and white people just don't get it here. I can't trust them or understand them, so they ain't my friends. They're not enemies, well, not most of them … but they're not my friends" (646). This statement shows how racism affects the Black community's feelings towards the white community. Frequently, Black people feel the need to change how they act and hide their true feelings and identities towards others out of fear of discrimination. Disparities affect the abilities of the two extremes, those affected and those not, to connect socially and emotionally.

Similarly, discrimination has been shown to create mental challenges for people of color. Discrimination has been shown to cause a lot of stress for people of color, manifesting itself in other ways inside the individual or forcing them to find ways to cope and deal with the stress. Arkin et al. writes that institutionalized racism "could lead to chronic anxiety and worry about whether personal incidents will occur and, potentially, because it reflects social exclusion, hatred or lack of respect for one's racial or ethnic group" (175). This information shows how this racism can create disorders and adverse feelings about oneself and their community. People have many different strategies to cope with unhealthy mental states, such as therapy, yoga, and exercise. However, a study conducted on the stressors that mothers experience found, "moms took to smoking to cope with [stress] while others chose suppression" (Rizzieri 6). This shows that the Black community has been burdened with the pressure and stress of anxiety, and is not utilizing healthy coping strategies to combat it. The unjust laws imposed on people of color affect their mental states by creating negative attitudes and thinking, depression, anxiety, and stress that will go on to affect how they live their lives and potentially their health.

Likewise, the many different inequalities that are created by systemic racism affect the lives of people of color physically. Inequity has been associated with the decline of the health of Black communities. Author Tyson Brown states, "there has been a growing recognition that the fundamental cause of health inequalities along racial lines is structural racism, which involves systemic racial exclusion from power, resources, opportunities, and well-being that is embedded in social institutions" (1). Here, Brown explains how the effects of racism, like fewer resources and opportunities, negatively affect the health of people of color. With fewer opportunities, Black people are disadvantaged in educational systems which does not allow them to access better-paying jobs. By having fewer resources like income, they cannot afford healthy foods, healthcare, better education, and adequate living spaces. As previously mentioned, racism increases the chances of smoking which itself is a risk factor for endless diseases. With minimal governmental representation, they also lack the power to change these issues for themselves, creating a cycle of damage to their health and society.

Nonetheless, others believe that inequality is a good thing and that creating equality amongst all people will only be harmful rather than beneficial for the community. Some people believe certain restorative policies will hurt the economy and its people with extreme decreases in job opportunities and income stating, "[A] radical mandated wage policy and one-size-fits-all regulations will lead to fewer employment opportunities, less economic freedom, [and] restricted hours for workers" (qtd. in Davidson). This quote by Republican Representative Frederick B. Keller implies that creating equality would harm the economy rather than improve it. Additionally, others believe inequality is not necessarily a bad thing. According to economist Alan B. Krueger in *Inequality Reader: Contemporary & Foundational Reading in Race, Class, & Gender,* inequality creates "incentives for individuals to work hard, invest, and innovate" (23). This quote implies that disparities help the economy by creating motivation in society's workers to do better. They argue that the best thing for the economy is to create a balance between the good and bad that comes with inequity.

Although equality may change the economy and lower employment privileges for certain groups of people, it is important to remember that inequality itself creates economic differences between different groups of people, which should not be overlooked. In "Systemic and Structural Racism: Definitions, Examples, Health Damages, and Approaches to Dismantling," Elaine Arkin explains these inequities not only harm the health and well-being of minority groups with below-average resources and options, but also by limiting "the next generation's employment, and hence their economic opportunities—for example, through poorly resourced schools" (175). She is explaining that disparities affect these communities in many different aspects of their lives, including economically. It is not enough just to say that creating equality will ruin the economic system when its opposite does the same and worse to the marginalized groups it attacks. Inequality itself does not create incentives to do better in life, but it is its consequences that cause people of color to innovate, find new sources of income, and work hard in endless shifts to simply provide the bare minimum for themselves and their families. Implying that inequality is a motivational drive is sugarcoating the real issue of the disproportionate harsh reality that forces people of color to work ten times harder than white Americans to live in a nation that tears them down on a daily basis. Disparities are harmful, not helpful, and should be removed to create a better democracy.

For these reasons, a drastic change needs to occur in the United States government. One solution would be to reform legislation as a whole, especially those that have been harming people of color. For example, Davidson writes, "The Fairness for Farm Workers Act, … was reintroduced last month and would phase out the FLSA overtime exemption for agricultural workers." This example aims to reform the New Deal to change its discriminatory effects. Besides improving the laws that create disadvantages, these laws could be completely removed since they create and promote inequity. The government can also work to create new laws that will combat the disparities and benefit minority groups. If the problem is the laws that are in place that allow for inequality and mistreatment of minority communities, correcting these laws would be a step in the right direction for reducing these imbalances.

Secondly, the implementation of more and better political representation in governmental systems can help reduce inequality. The government of the United States is a democracy, meaning the people hold the power. However, the power is held within the governmental branches and the citizens must vote on whom they would like to fill these governmental branches. According to Arkin, "Lack of political power produces lack of access to key resources and opportunities needed to be healthy, such as clean water, pollution-free neighborhoods, well-resourced schools, affordable housing, and access to medical care" (175). The quote shows how having the proper representation is crucial in obtaining needed resources. In creating more diverse legal representation, the chances of lawful discrimination will be reduced because there will be advocates with the voice and power to stand up for minorities and implement changes in laws, as previously discussed. In obtaining a better and more diverse representation, there will be a greater chance for racial disparities to be addressed because there will be individuals with stronger motives to address and reform these issues and prevent more from forming.

Lastly, there needs to be more public awareness and education on these issues. Things like white ignorance need to be addressed and dismantled as "it denies the possibility of racist bias and erases the possibility of racism" (Damien and Tate 143). In the attempt to avoid discrimination, things that explain away racism need to stop as they block the beginning steps of acknowledging and acceptance of racism. The public should be educated on this issue and the corresponding laws that encompass and fuel it. Without a greater understanding and knowledge surrounding the topic, change cannot be achieved. Some schools have already begun this process by "educating themselves, critically reflecting on their attitudes and behavior, having difficult and at times confrontational conversations about race, and by crafting and implementing race-policies and procedures" (Brooks 636). These efforts can make a significant difference in the lives of the students involved and how they go on to view the world. People cannot be expected to change something they do not know about. Therefore, the more aware people are of the issues, the more change can result from it.

In short, legislation sets the standard for how people under its control are treated. If the government allows for discrimination through its policies, discrimination will be implemented. These laws manifest themselves as racism throughout organizations creating imbalances in court and justice systems, employment, housing, education, income, healthcare, and wellness. Consequently, governmental reforms, diverse advocacy, and nationwide recognition of systemic oppression are the key components to successfully overcoming this mistake of the past. As House of Representatives member Alma Adams states, "We cannot build a more equitable future for this country without first confronting the active legacy of slavery throughout our institutions … and recognizing the federal government's continued role in perpetuating racial discrimination" (Davidson).

Works Cited

Arkin, Elaine, Paula A. Braveman, Nicole Holm, Tina Kauh, and Dwayne Proctor. "Systemic and Structural Racism: Definitions, Examples, Health Damages, and Approaches to Dismantling." *Health Affairs,* vol. 41, no. 2, 7 Feb. 2022, pp. 171–178, https://doi.org/https://doi.org/10.1377/hlthaff.2021.01394.

Brooks, Jeffrey S., and Terri N. Watson. "School Leadership and Racism: An Ecological Perspective." *Urban Education,* vol. 54, no. 5, 10 July 2018, pp. 631–655, https://doi.org/10.1177/0042085918783821.

Brown, Tyson H., and Patricia A. Homan. "Frontiers in Measuring Structural Racism and Its Health Effects." *Health Services Research,* vol. 57, no. 3, June 2022, pp. 443–47. https://doi.org/10.1111/1475-6773.13978.

Davidson, Joe. "Democrats Push to Undo New Deal's Racist Aspects." *Washington Post,* 13 June 2021.

Krueger, Alan B. "Chapter 4: Inequality, Too Much of a Good Thing." *Inequality Reader: Contemporary & Foundational Readings in Race, Class, & Gender,* edited by David B. Grusky and Szonja Szelenyi, Westview Press, 2006, pp. 23–31.

Page, Damien, and Shirley Anne Tate. "Whiteliness and Institutional Racism: Hiding behind (Un)Conscious Bias." *Ethics and Education,* vol. 13, no. 1, 2018, pp. 141–55. https://doi.org/10.1080/17449642.2018.1428718.

"Racial Disparities Persist in Many U.S. Jails." *The Pew Charitable Trusts,* 16 May 2023, www.pewtrusts.org/en/research-and-analysis/issue-briefs/2023/05/racial-disparities-persist-in-many-us-jails.

Rizzieri, Ashley, and Mayra Rodriguez, and Denisia N. Thomas. "Underlying Pressures That Black Mothers and Their Children Face: A Qualitative Assessment on the Effects of Racism/Discrimination and the Covid 19 Pandemic." medRxiv, Cold Spring Harbor Laboratory Press, 23 Feb. 2023, doi.org/10.1101/2023.02.15.23286011.

"The Court Abandons Voting Rights." *New York Times,* 2 July 2021, p. A20 (L).

Questions to Consider

1. Destiny mentions in her reflection that it was challenging to decide "which points were worth discussing even though they all felt equally important," which can be the case with a topic that is carefully researched. Looking through the paper, how do you think this writer made choices about organizational strategies and what to tell the reader first, second, and third? What information does the reader need to have at the beginning in order to understand the rest of the argument? How does background information fit into a research-based argument and how might that be based on audience?

2. Counterarguments, or showing another side to an issue, is an important part of creating an effective argument, but how that looks may be different depending upon the issue under investigation. Destiny mentioned that it was challenging to find a counterargument, but she managed to do so as part of her research. What is the counterargument she presents in this essay? How does she address that differing perspective? What other contrary ideas or counterarguments might exist that could also be addressed in this paper?

3. This research-based argument takes on a large, systemic issue, offering history, outlining the problem, and suggesting possible solutions. How does this writer integrate outside information to support her argument? What rhetorical appeals can you identify in this essay? In your opinion, which ones are the most compelling and why?

Category: Rhetorical Analysis

The next genre of writing we will explore is the Rhetorical Analysis, which is a type of analytic approach for interpreting texts that focuses on rhetorical appeals and how they persuade an audience. As discussed in the "Rhetorical Terms and Appeals" section near the beginning of this book, the study of rhetoric entails examining persuasive texts in order to understand how they work. In a rhetorical analysis, you will be asked to analyze texts—which could be magazine ads, editorials, political speeches, images, videos, newspaper articles, commercials, or a host of other types of texts—from a rhetorical perspective.

While students often have background with textual analysis prior to coming to college, many first-year writers report that rhetorical analysis is a new genre for them. Because of that, examples of this type of essay may be helpful to you so that you can get an idea of what might be expected in an analysis of this sort. Although your instructor may have specific guidelines and types of assignments that are different from the examples you see here, all rhetorical analysis essays ask the writer to investigate a text to see how it operates rhetorically. You might consider aspects of a text such as pathos (how the text moves the emotions of the audience), ethos (the authority or character of the speaker/writer), and logos (how logically an argument is presented), as well as the timing of the text you are critiquing (kairos), the events or pressures that caused the text to arise (exigence), the context in which it was published or distributed, the audience for which it was intended, the style or tone it takes in order to connect with the audience, etc. By engaging in rhetorical analysis, you will become more aware of the rhetorical texts around you in your everyday life and be able to discern the ways in which you are persuaded. Additionally, through this awareness, you can learn to craft more rhetorically effective texts yourself, as you will when you create various arguments as part of your classroom assignments.

You may hear terms in your first-year writing classes such as "rhetorical situation" or "rhetorical triangle." These concepts are a way of imagining the complex relationship of rhetorical texts and the context(s) in which they arise. While these analytic tools may represent simple versions of the relationships that occur in rhetorical interactions—for instance, considering aspects such as message, audience, and rhetor—they can be more complex to include shaping elements of rhetorical texts, such as genre, exigencies, medium, distribution, reception, circulation, and many others. Rhetorical texts do not arise in a vacuum—they both shape and are shaped by the people, events, pressures, controversies, ideas, and cultural norms in which they arise, and are further shaped by the affordances and constraints of mediums, genre, and methods of

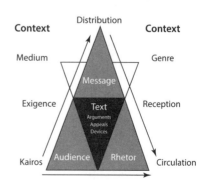

distribution or circulation. (For instance, a rhetorical text created for a scholarly journal will be composed very differently than one created in order to be circulated on social media.) In a nutshell, rhetoric is a very complex practice, so to analyze it requires more than being able to simply identify the main argument or the rhetorical appeals at play, though those are definitely part of the work of rhetorical analysis, too.

In our upcoming section of student work, you will see analyses of texts from multiple mediums and genres, demonstrating the range of texts that may be the subject of rhetorical analysis. Similarly, each student has chosen to focus on different aspects of their chosen texts and to approach their rhetorical analyses from various perspectives. For complex texts, it can be difficult to decide which elements to include and which to exclude, as it could be possible to do an in-depth analysis that was significantly longer than your assignments for first-year writing will allow. As with other assignments, it may be challenging to "narrow down" the scope of your analysis to focus on the most interesting, relevant, or striking rhetorical elements in your text, so these essays could provide you with a useful example to follow.

Our D'Artagnan Award winner for Rhetorical Analysis is Nadia Leontescu for her essay "Living Life More Fully: A Rhetorical Analysis," which examines an Instagram marketing video produced by Xavier. Her essay analyzes both overt and subtle messages in this multimodal text, including the effects of sound and lighting, movement, and camera angles in addition to other elements. Our judges were impressed by Nadia's "sophisticated analysis," which highlights how a combination of devices works together to create an effective rhetorical text. This is an especially interesting analysis because, as students at Xavier, it offers the opportunity for reflection on the texts that have also worked to influence your decisions and choices about college.

Our next essay is a rhetorical analysis by Olivia Neiss entitled "An Analysis of the Argument Against School Uniforms." Olivia's essay examines how a newspaper opinion piece, which argues against mandatory school uniforms, combines rhetorical appeals in complex ways to create a compelling argument. Readers found Olvia's "strong, clear analysis" to be an exemplar of the type of rhetorical analysis that students are often asked to do, where they might look closely at a source that they are using as part of a research process. While Olivia does not use the names of the traditional rhetorical appeals (ethos, pathos, logos) she clearly describes how each of these works in this text.

The third essay in this category is by Jacob Thacker for his "'This Is America'" Analysis." His essay, which focuses on the ethical implications of race, violence, and power in Childish Gambino's "This is America" song and video, is also the only essay in the Rhetorical Analysis category to carry the D'Artagnan Insignia for Advocacy in Action. Analyzing the intersection between music, lyrics, sound, and video, Jacob creates a powerful essay that asks the audience to think more deeply about social justice issues as they follow along with his examination. Readers noted that this essay "models close reading of a video and does so in a way that is compelling and vivid to a reader even if they haven't seen the video."

Our final essay in the Rhetorical Analysis category is "Hope for a Nation: A Rhetorical Analysis of Barack Obama's 2004 DNC Speech" by Nick Viola. Political speeches, because they have the potential for great social influence, are an important site for rhetorical analysis and this essay effectively dissects a political speech, showing how it can deeply affect listeners. Readers found Nicks' essay to be particularly well-focused and were impressed that it "moves beyond just ethos/pathos/logos, making good use of textual evidence."

In each of these rhetorical analysis essays, you will see how student writers examine texts through a rhetorical lens, showing how persuasion works in various mediums. As you read these works, you can get a sense of how applying the tools of rhetorical analysis can deepen your understanding of the texts you encounter, whether they are videos, political speeches, articles, or trailers. As you become more familiar with rhetoric and how it works, you will start to see many kinds of "persuasive texts" in the world around you. The tools you develop through rhetorical analysis can assist you in deepening your understanding of how those texts work to change your mind, alter your perceptions, or move you to act in particular ways. An ability to see the workings of persuasion can allow you to step back from these devices to make clearer decisions based on your own logic, values, and ethics, as well as deepen the meaning of the many texts you encounter in your day-to-day life.

Living Life More Fully: A Rhetorical Analysis

Nadia Leontescu
D'Artagnan Award Winner for Rhetorical Analysis

Reflection

At first when my professor assigned us the task of rhetorically analyzing an artifact related to Xavier, I had a bit of a difficult time figuring out what I wanted to do. There are posters and advertisements for things all around campus, yet there were not many that grabbed my attention or struck up any ideas. I first thought I was going to be able to analyze one of the research posters I pass by all the time in Albers Hall, but I found my initial ideas to be shallow, and I didn't feel I had enough analysis to thoroughly discuss. Then, after reading some of the essays in *The Write Path,* I realized that I didn't have to look for something written, I could use visual media! Then I got to thinking, where could I find videos that related to Xavier? Then it hit: the Xavier Instagram page. I had seen so many videos on there, and I eventually found one that I felt confident in analyzing that used a variety of appeals and techniques.

From there, I was really able to get ideas on the page. Usually when I'm tasked with writing a paper, I immediately go to writing an outline. No matter the subject, I've found that outlining is what takes the bulk of my time and is the way in which I can organize my ideas so that it aids future me in writing the paper. So, after watching the video a few times and jotting down the main techniques employed, I was able to start forming arguments, analysis, and an organization to the outline. While I had a thesis after the preliminary viewings, during the writing and revision processes I, like I usually do, ended up editing this thesis based on how my ideas flowed in the paper and what I truly write about. Like I said, outlining for me tends to take longer than writing the paper itself, mainly because I outline almost every idea/claim, evidence I'll use to back it up, and the analysis of that evidence; from there, I pretty much just take those ideas and make them flow in a succinct, thorough paragraph that ties everything together. Once I write out the whole paper, I tend to go back on my own and revise any spelling and grammar issues, taking some time away from it so I can go back with fresh eyes to determine if the content needs to be changed. Peer review also helps with this, as I like to use what others say to ensure I make the most sense and make claims that are backed up thoroughly.

Living Life More Fully: A Rhetorical Analysis

In the age of technology, I—like many others—find myself scrolling through social media pages to look for pertinent information, especially during important times like my college search. Sure, college websites have plenty of information on what majors and clubs there were, admissions timelines, and pretty much the answers to most of the typical questions prospective college students are asking. However, when I wanted to see what the experiences were really like at these colleges, I looked to Instagram. Photos of activities, events, sports, announcements, all of the things that make the college experience—that's what I was really looking for. Thus, it has become very important for colleges to put out engaging social media content that is applicable to a wide range of audiences. In light of the new year, Xavier University recently posted a short semi-promotional video with the caption "Our resolution this year? Live more fully"[1] on their Instagram page in order to add to the "More Xavier" initiative. It is essentially a compilation of various scenes displaying student life with a motivational narrative behind it. In the video, the creators are able to establish both pathos and ethos through the use of audio, visual, and narrative techniques, creating an emotional appeal as well as a sense of credibility and familiarization with the audience.

The first thing the viewer notices at the beginning is the backing sounds and music, which helps establish the energy of the video and draw the viewer in. It starts with solely the tick of a metronome until a fast paced, short stroke orchestral piece comes in. Both the tempo and sound of this background create a sense of urgency and high energy with the audience. It is almost a dramatic choice, not to emphasize a certain drama about the video, but to create a feeling that the audience should keep watching in a sort of suspense. As the metronome ticks continue with the music, viewers are not only given a sense of urgency, but some form of stability and steadiness as well. While the metronome is at a quicker pace, it is a repetitive beat that does not change, providing the viewer with a grounding energy to pair with the higher energy of the music itself. As the metronome fades and more instruments and sounds are added, everything starts to build to give movement to the video. It builds up the suspense, keeping the energy high while the audience awaits more scenes to play through, each one also building in energy. The music is full, reminding the viewer that life should be lived fully and that at Xavier, life can have that same fullness and energy.

As the video continues, it integrates a mix of unique scenes that all contribute to a particular mood created to induce an emotional appeal for the viewer. The brightness of each scene gives an energetic and happy mood, and the color scheme goes along with this as well. The colors remain fairly light and there are no scenes with dark or intense lighting, shying away from any sad, angry, or overall dark connotations. Most of the subjects are either visibly smiling or excited about what they are doing, contributing to the general joyfulness of the video. There are also scenes in which the subjects are more focused or somber, such as the scene with Father Eric or the two women in the lab. All of these techniques allow the viewer not only to feel the excitement from this college experience, but also the seriousness and focus that comes with it. The variety of emotions can appeal to various audiences depending on the mood they connect with most strongly when it comes to the idea of college.

[1] Xavier University (@xavieruniversity), "Our resolution this year? Live more fully.", Instagram, video, January 5, 2024, www.instagram.com/reel/C1vJJ3vOx7i/?utm_source =ig_web_copy_link&igsh=MzRlODBiNWFlZA=.

Along with a variety of emotional appeals depicted through each scene, the creators are also able to create a sense of "realness" and trust with the viewer in each scene and subject. By shooting the video on location—Xavier's campus— it allows the audience to see that it is a legitimate college environment and aids in an audience connection to the scene. As a promo for a college, prospective students and parents want to see a variety of activities and experiences available; therefore, demonstrating a mix of the excitement that comes with sports and extracurriculars, focus of academics, joy of seeing friends, and enjoyment of campus helps contribute to the credibility and "realness" of the message and the college itself. The scenes show all real experiences, utilizing camera techniques to 'follow' each subject and display what they are doing in the moment to allow the viewer to feel like they are a part of it. These techniques also help the viewer clearly see the facial expressions and body language of the subjects, not only adding to the emotional appeal but also establishing a sense of trust and rapport with the audience. The diversity in scenes and subjects allows for the audience to get a feel that Xavier provides a diverse environment with many ways to "live more fully," and that they are credible in discussing this initiative.

This theme to live more fully—and that it can be done at Xavier—is accentuated with the narration, the creators continuing the mix of pathos and ethos in order to appeal to a wider range of audiences. The repetition of the narrator discussing living "more truthfully," "… more faithfully," "… more mindfully," etc. addresses this theme directly. This narration and repetition often directly tie into what the scenes are showing, emphasizing the message, and giving credibility to Xavier as the institution to live out that message. While the experience or message is being described, it is also visually presented to demonstrate that at Xavier, it is not just stated but done. It connects emotionally with the audience, creating an image for them of their own possible experiences there and what life could look like. Certain word choices such as "take in" or "discover" within this context help add to this imagined future as well. This wording inspires future thinking, especially appealing to possible future students or even current ones to explore what Xavier has to offer. It emphasizes that Xavier has the opportunities, if only you can imagine yourself there. The narrator's tone and own emotion also facilitates the emotional sway, remaining focused on the topics at hand but also audibly happy and energetic. Even though the narrator cannot be seen, they add to the already established energy and emotion of the video, creating another auditory component that helps appeal to the viewers. When they see smiling faces while hearing the happiness in the narration, it strengthens the influence of the message no matter the audience.

The audio, visual and narrative choices by the creators of this promotional video aid in employing pathos and ethos appeals to the audience, forming emotional connections, familiarity, and credibility. The interplay between every choice allows the creators to effectively influence various targeted audiences, whether future students, parents, current students, etc. They have also chosen to use the video in the home page of their website, further demonstrating the use for a broader audience. The video gets the message across—especially in a timely manner as it related to the New Year and was posted around that time frame—meanwhile appealing rhetorically to the audience. It inspires one to live life fully, promoting Xavier as the place to do that no matter who you are or what your goals are. It's important to know your audience and use your platform responsibly, and this video and its influence demonstrates the importance in drawing future college students in to show not only Xavier as an opportunity for something greater, but for college in general as an opportunity to explore who you are and what you want your life to become.

Work Cited

Xavier University (@xavieruniversity). "Our resolution this year? Live more fully." Instagram, video, January 5, 2024, www.instagram.com/reel/C1vJJ3vOx7i/?utm_source=ig_web_copy_link&igsh=M zRlODBiNWFlZA=.

Questions to Consider

1. In the second paragraph, Nadia closely analyzes the effects of music in the video she is analyzing. When you encounter multimodal arguments that include sound, how consciously do you note how those sounds affect your perception of that text? What sounds do you find appealing or off-putting? Think of a multimodal argument that includes music or sound that you find appealing: what specific sounds, tempos, music, or audio effects move you in certain ways? How can sound amplify or reinforce other modes of persuasion, such as text and visual images?

2. Nadia's thesis is clear, specific, and makes an analytic claim about the text she is examining. How does this thesis statement forecast what is coming up in the rest of the essay? Do you think it accurately portrays the contents of this analysis and makes an argument about how the text operates rhetorically? How can you adapt her technique or approach to creating an effective thesis statement for a rhetorical analysis paper that you might write?

3. Choosing a college to attend is a big decision for many young people, who are presented with competing messages and persuasive texts trying to convince them to take a particular educational path. As Xavier students, what persuaded you to attend Xavier? What other competing institutional messages did you encounter while making your decision about the college you would attend? What was it about Xavier's message that persuaded you to attend this specific university? What rhetorical appeals did you find convincing about Xavier's messages, campus, people, or materials?

An Analysis of the Argument Against School Uniforms

Olivia Neiss
Honorable Mention for Rhetorical Analysis

Reflection

When assigned a rhetorical analysis, I carefully thought about my topic. I wanted a topic I do not hear many people talk about, thus landing on school uniforms. I began looking for articles and chose one that argued a perspective I had not heard before. I then started forming my outline to move chronologically. After my outline, I decided to start with my introduction because I knew it would help me set the intention for my paper and keep the direction focused. The first body paragraph came very easily to me as I knew I wanted to start by explaining the story the author had used and work from there. I was able to pick up on the smaller details in wording and placement that I found intriguing as they made the author's article resonate with me more.

After moving through peer-review, finishing my final draft, and a trip to the Writing Center, I felt that I had a strong sense of direction for my final draft. I knew that I could delve deeper for each claim, really dissecting and understanding the way the author argued his point. My visit to the Writing Center was particularly impactful in my revision and I found myself making more than just structural and wording adjustments. I reconsidered my evaluations of each portion of the argument, providing more detail, and even fully changing my opinion about the end of the article. I would advise others to visit the Writing Center whether you are struggling with the assignment or not. At the Writing Center, they help you carefully think about your writing so that you can make your own changes. After I felt my final draft was complete, I went back through it to check for any grammar mistakes I might have missed. Overall, it was a stressful but rewarding process as I paced through my analysis of André Spicer's article "Not Even Bankers Wear Ties and Blazers. So Why Should School Children?"

An Analysis of the Argument Against School Uniforms

The education we receive in our youth sets the trajectory of our lives. While our primary education is a center for academics, it is also a time to begin understanding ourselves as we learn how to interact with others, discover our interests, and how we want to express ourselves. However, as school uniforms have become increasingly popularized, it is easy to question how they affect both academic and social learning. André Spicer writes for *The Guardian*, "Not Even Bankers Wear Ties and Blazers. So Why Should School Children?" In this article, he argues against school uniforms from an uncommon perspective, emphasizing the fact that children in school have stricter and more constraining dress codes than many adults in the business world. Utilizing personal stories, observations, facts and statistics, and debunking many preconceived notions,

Spicer's article aims to convince readers that school uniforms may be overly strict, harsh, and potentially detrimental to students and their families. With this article, Spicer seeks to encourage schools to allow for more self-expression.

To introduce his argument, Spicer uses personal stories and observations explained through intentionally emotional language. Spicer drops his daughter off at school in her tie, blazer, and skirt, "[squirming] with discomfort." Afterward, he heads to work, where he is "surrounded by bankers" wearing open-necked shirts with a lack of a tie and blazer. This observational story from Spicer establishes his credibility to speak on the topic of school uniforms. As Spicer is a professor at the Bayes Business School at City, University of London, he regularly sees bankers and businessmen. Because he has a daughter who attends a school in which uniforms are required, he is also witness to how students may be affected by uniforms. It is also worth noting that Spicer's choice of words, "surrounded by bankers," proves that Spicer can argue the topic by comparing school uniforms to those of bankers and businessmen.

Additionally, Spicer's usage of the words "squirmed" and "discomfort" imply that the uniform is uncomfortable for his daughter, leading the reader to assume that other students feel this discomfort as well. Spicer's intended audience is most likely other parents. Therefore, painting a picture of children being uncomfortable in their school clothes evokes feelings of distress and concern that may resonate with parents more so than people without children. By starting his argument with observable facts and emotional appeals, Spicer intentionally makes it difficult for readers to disagree with his argument.

Through specific examples, Spicer directs his argument toward the severity of the punishments that students face for being out of dress code. He explains that his daughter was "one of the lucky ones" because she was given "special dispensation" to take off her uniform blazer due to the weather, but that other kids may not be so lucky. He calls on stories of students being given detention for taking off their uniform blazers in "sweltering heat" and other students "being excluded from class for wearing the wrong kind of sock." In doing so, he demonstrates the ways in which children are being excessively punished and even deprived of learning due to actions that are recognizably minuscule. Spicer continues to use persuasive diction when using the word "sweltering" to describe the outside temperature. Such vivid language not only creates a scene for the reader but also elicits a sense of empathy for kids who are forced to feel uncomfortable due to their uniforms. In order for this portion of his argument to be effective, Spicer needs readers to believe that taking off blazers and wearing the wrong socks are excusable actions, even if they are direct violations of the dress code. In order to do this, he highlights how such strict dress codes can be harmful to students' education, knocking down a symbolic pillar supporting the justification that school uniforms are necessary to student success.

After appealing to the emotions of the reader, Spicer effectively begins to build his argument using statistics. He states that most schools justify the policies with the claim that uniforms "help to prepare children for the 'real world' of work." He then goes on to provide numbers that suggest that the dress code schools are preparing students for, no longer exists. These statistics include approximately 5% of workplaces having uniforms, the sales of more formal work attire decreasing by 40% in the last five years, and a survey that found that 92% of people believe it to be acceptable to go to work without a tie. He also mentions that Elon Musk and Mark Zuckerburg, two of the most famous businessmen in the world, are consistently seen wearing casual attire. Because not everyone sees businessmen and bankers every day, they are required to rely on Spicer's perspective of how they dress for work. However, by detailing Musk and Zuckerburg, Spicer creates a connection and mental image of the face of today's business world so that this section of his argument connects with all readers. Spicer uses these facts to persuade readers that the primary justification for uniforms is proving to be weak. Incorporating numbers into an already emotional argument provides strength and solidity. While readers can potentially disregard the emotional appeals Spicer uses, it is considerably harder to ignore numbers.

Spicer compellingly develops his argument further, leaning on studies to disprove another common justification used for the implementation of school uniforms. Spicer explains that the true reason for such policies is rooted in the belief that students will behave and perform better in uniform rather than out of uniform. Using a survey published in Public Health Reviews, Spicer explains that uniforms do aid in the management of students but that there is no solid evidence supporting the claim that uniforms lead to better academic performance from students. Spicer has intentionally included this fact knowing it may work against his argument to show that he acknowledges that there are also positives to uniforms. Admitting when the other side of the argument has a fair claim establishes credibility as the audience will trust that Spicer is providing all the necessary aspects of the argument rather than presenting a biased, one-sided defense. Spicer also includes negative results found by the study that do not directly dispute the claim that uniforms lead to better performing students, explaining that the study also found that uniforms have negative impacts on student health because of the physical restriction caused by uniforms. It is for girls that this restriction is more impactful as they are often required to wear skirts. Again, Spicer uses facts alongside the emotional appeals to bolster his argument.

Spicer continues to use the method of introducing a popular belief then using facts and statistics to disprove the claim. Toward the end of his article, he discusses the ideas of inclusion and tradition that many use to justify uniform dress codes. To dispute these claims, Spicer first explains that students who do not fit the "outdated [mold]," such as non-binary students and those with sensory sensitivities, can potentially feel ostracized rather than included. This creates the idea that students would feel more comfortable in the clothing they choose. To the claim on tradition, Spicer explains that uniforms only started spreading through schools in the early 20th century and became stricter in 1987 with the outlawing of corporal punishment in schools. While it may be compelling to assume or claim that custom dating back to the early 20th century has grounds to be considered tradition, the thought is quickly masked by the mention of corporal punishment. The mention of corporal punishment is strategic as it links uniforms to a widely unaccepted form of punishment for children. By claiming uniforms to be a replacement of such a punishment pushes the idea that uniforms are harmful, almost as if they are a punishment in themselves. This also creates a connection to the punishments students received that Spicer had previously discussed, reinforcing both the current and former claims.

Concluding his argument, Spicer gives his own solution to the problem he has introduced, creating a very strong defense. To truly prepare children for "real world" work attire, Spicer suggests that schools should set broad guidelines for children, allowing them to dress and express themselves. Denouncing an "outdated one-size fits all rulebook," he claims we need to "challenge the invented tradition" of uniforms and adopt a modern perspective. Calling uniforms "outdated" urges readers to feel that harsh dress codes for children should become a thing of the past. Because uniforms have become so prominent, taking a stance against them sets Spicer up to appear as if he is merely complaining. However, furnishing a specific solution demonstrates that he has scrutinized his own argument thoroughly enough to provide a solution he believes justifies the issue. Additionally, it revokes an individual's ability to claim that Spicer's argument is a series of griping. While it is a small detail, it provides a significant amount of support to his argument.

Spicer introduces his argument, immediately catering towards the emotions of readers. He quickly switches tactics, incorporating stats to disprove common beliefs about school uniforms and the current appropriate work attire. While relying heavily on facts and agreed-upon truths, Spicer builds a case in which the cons of uniforms outweigh the pros. Spicer's method of introducing and then dismantling a claim is effective. He speaks on numerous perspectives and arguments while also acknowledging where the positives to uniforms exist. His ending is strong as he supplies a direction he believes schools should take to diminish the harm school uniforms can inflict. Spicer's argument is unique and is undeniably effective due to his use of both emotional and logical appeals to the reader.

Work Cited

Spicer, André. "Not Even Bankers Wear Ties and Blazers Any More. So Why Should Schoolchildren?" *The Guardian*, 25 September 2023, www.theguardian.com/commentisfree/2023/sep/25/why-do-we-force-our-kids-into-ties-and-blazers-when-not-even-bankers-wear-them-any-more.

Questions to Consider

1. Rhetorical analyses closely examine the rhetorical appeals, strategies, and devices deployed by a text in order to understand how a text works to persuade. Although Olivia does not use the terms ethos, pathos, and logos, her analysis still covers these areas. Looking through her paper, can you identify where she is analyzing each of these appeals? What words does she use to indicate these appeals so that readers know that is what is under consideration?

2. Olivia mentions that she organized her initial outline to move chronologically through the text. When looking at her finished paper, what other organizational strategies can you discern? What does each paragraph "do" for her overall paper? How is she grouping or organizing the areas of the text under analysis?

3. Going to the Writing Center was important to Olivia's composing process and she notes that it had a big impact on her paper beyond structural and wording adjustments. How might Olivia's paper have been different or less effective with fewer details or analysis? What might have been missed if she had not had feedback from peer tutors at the Writing Center? What benefits might writers receive by learning to see their writing differently?

"This Is America" Analysis

Jacob Thacker
Honorable Mention for Rhetorical Analysis

Reflection

Starting on my analysis paper, I was drawn to dissect the song and music video of "This Is America." My fascination with music and the song's social justice undertones propelled me to explore the myriad interpretations it sparked upon its release. This journey of analysis was a testament to the power of music and its ability to ignite societal discourse. Childish Gambino, one of my favorite artists, also made me want to investigate the meaning of the song/video even further.

The most challenging part of this assignment was condensing the analysis after writing the paper. After completing my first draft, I realized I was around 4000 words and had to condense the paper heavily to make it more concise. It was easy to overanalyze with the music video for the song. Somebody could analyze the video further than I did in the essay to keep it concise, with many references and allusions throughout it. When composing the paper, I analyzed the video and song together in sections to keep the narrative progressive. Writing for both the lyrical and visual sides of the song, I wrote the analysis of scenes at different times. I would take breaks, reread what I had written before, and rewatch/listen to what I had written about up to that point. Once I finished my first draft of the paper, I took it to some other people to review what I had already written and get their thoughts on what I should change/remove from the paper. I drafted the paper to cover the points I wanted within the song/video.

Try to spread out the time when you write and read other texts on the subject you are writing about. Reading other people's works on a topic can help you realize things you might want to add, remove, or expand upon within your paper. Getting other perspectives from other people is essential for my writing process, and running your papers by other people to get feedback and thoughts can be very beneficial to the writing process and let you gain other perspectives on your paper.

Content Warning

This essay contains an analysis of a text that deals with gun violence and suicide.

"This Is America" Analysis

On Sunday, May 6th, 2018, the song, and music video for "This Is America" debuted. The song was performed the previous night on "Saturday Night Live" for the first time. The performance provided little indication of the profound and provocative themes depicted in the accompanying music video, shocking audiences upon its debut the following day. "This is America" builds anticipation through unexpected lyrics and videos that emphasize the themes and points of the song through the usage of pathos and ethos in lyrical and visual form.

Donald Glover, who goes by the stage name "Childish Gambino," is known for his all-around success and multi-faceted interests, journeying into various art forms with music, film, and acting. Even musically, he has shifted between genres, going from hip hop/rap in his first two albums "Camp" and "Because the Internet" to an R&B theme in his third album "Awaken My Love!" before the release of "This Is America." Entering one of his songs, it is hard to know what to expect, adding to the audience's feeling of anticipation at the song's start.

The emotional nature of the melody and beat of "This is America" creates interest in seeing what will happen next. The song and video have soft choral singing and guitar strums to start, but that shifts into a hard-hitting trap beat after the first few moments of the music. The video creates even more unease for the audience with the change of tone in the beginning before the instrumental change. The video starts with an image of an empty warehouse with a chair holding a guitar. A man walks up to the chair, sits, and begins to play the guitar as the camera shakily pans around the support beams in the warehouse into view of Glover standing straight in the center of the room. The camera shaking adds to the unease of the beginning, where it is hard to know what to expect, which continues throughout the song and video.

The video establishes Glover's ethos, with his perspective constantly changing. Glover starts to dance while making different facial expressions that look in pain or confusion, which appeals to the audience's feeling of unease at the start of the video. As he continues to dance, the camera continues to pan back to where the man was playing guitar, where his head is now wrapped with a bag, and he is no longer playing the guitar. This continues to appeal to the audience's emotions with how confusing this is going along with the snippets of the trap beat sneaking into the soft chorus and guitar in the background. As the camera continues to pan, Glover dances over behind the man and reaches behind himself to pull out a pistol and shoot the sitting man in the head.

The audience's dramatic and emotional reaction to the shooting is purposely creating emotional pathos and ethos to tell the story. With the gunshot, the song's instrumental switches into the trap beat. This scene creates emotion for the audience as it is shocking visually with the blood coming out of the man's head as the body falls to the floor but audibly as well with the switch to the trap beat with the gunshot. This intro also creates a sense of fear for the audience because of the shock and fear of what comes next in the song. The introductory scene in the video also appeals to the audience's sense of ethics by using the bag and killing the man. As the trap beat comes into the song, the main chorus starts and appeals to the audience's sense of ethics through its lyrical content, stating, "Don't catch you slippin' now," raising an ethical question on gun violence.

The logical argument for gun violence is represented following the start of the chorus, as a child comes out holding a red cloth to take the gun away from Glover. This is a commentary on how guns are treated in America. This appeals to the audience's ethics by making them question the way that guns are treated in America, creating the question of whether firearms are treated with more respect than people. The camera then pans backward shakenly while Glover starts moving towards the camera, and the body of the man who was shot is dragged away behind him. A man runs through the shot while a car drives in the background, and people are leaning out of the windows.

This scene of death and voyeurism evokes a sense of overwhelmingness for the audience with the massive number of things going on in the background, which is continuous throughout the video. The camera is heavily focused on the foreground, with Glover dancing with some schoolchildren, leaving everything in the background blurry and hard to see. Using the camera this way raises an ethical question to the audience on whether people distract themselves with music/celebrities from other issues. The video continues for the first verse, with the chaos ensuing behind Glover, where people run, fight, hold weapons, ride bikes, etc.

The lyrics of the first verse offer ethical questions to the audience, with "police be trippin' now" raising questions on police brutality and "guns in my area," bringing back the theme of gun violence. As the song moves back into the chorus, the video transitions into a new scene with a choir singing, "Get your money, black man," offering more ethical questions for the audience on how it is to be black in America. In the scene, the camera pans farther from the choir, where the wall opens, and Glover dances into the shot's foreground. He then gets handed an assault rifle and shoots the choir dead on the stage. This scene is shocking and raises more ethical questions on gun violence to the audience as the gun is handed away once again to a child with a red cloth while blood is still running down the wall in the background.

The acknowledgment of society's indifference is shown in the visuals of the dramatic departure of people. The chorus continues while the camera follows Glover as he walks away from the scene. People are running into the area with weapons, and the camera passes a police car. The camera then pans to a backshot of Glover as more people run in the background, with screams and gunshots echoing throughout the warehouse. The second verse starts with a moment of total silence while the chaos ensues in the background with a focused shot of Glover. Backup dancers then come into the scene, and the silence from the background noise continues. The dancing distracts from the background, raising the ethical question of covering up issues in America for the audience.

The impact of society's indifference and the violence of the situation is a dramatic focal point. In the video, a man is seen committing suicide by jumping off the second story of the warehouse as the chaos ensues, appealing again to the audience's sense of ethics and emotions. Lyrically, this section of the song also appeals to ethics with the lyrics "This a celly, that's a tool," which might be referencing Stephon Clark, who was shot by police officers who believed he had a weapon in his hand when it was just a phone. The video pans away from Glover after these lyrics up to the second floor, where people are seen recording the ongoing chaos beneath on their phones as it continues to pan back down the first floor in a wide shot. Glover is then seen dancing with the backup dancers while a figure in the background referencing the biblical version of death riding a horse receives a police escort through the warehouse. In the foreground, a car is burning, adding even more to the feeling of fear directed at the audience. As the verse continues, Gambino is centered in the shot and makes a hand gesture that mimics firing a gun, and all the backup dancers and people in the background run away as the song goes to silence.

Glover is attempting to show this storyline as his reality. When the last person is heard exiting, Gambino rests his hands while the silence continues. He lights a cigarette and walks to the right of the shot. This scene gives the audience a larger sense of fear because the inability to know what is coming next creates a sense of anxiety. The camera pans into the warehouse again, and Glover dances on a car as the chorus continues. The camera continues to pan backward into the darkness as the chorus ends, and silence and darkness ensue. With the silence, light drums come in with an eerie sound that sounds like screeching as the lyrics return.

As a black man, Glover is using his art to create the same amount of anxiety and trepidation with his video that he feels in real life; it is a manifestation. The camera pans to Glover running down a dimly lit hallway with the lyrics continuing, "You just a black man in this world, you just a barcode," offering more ethical questions for the audience on how no matter what a black man accomplishes, he is still just a black man in America. Glover sprints down the hallway into a dimly lit section where you can see the chasing white people. The video encapsulates the audience with one more ethical question with this scene through the use of the metaphor for the perpetuation of white supremacy in America. Glover has established his authority on the black experience and the emotion of anxiety for the audience, which is his lived experience.

Works Cited

Glover, Donald. "Childish Gambino: This is America." *YouTube,* uploaded by Donald Glover, 6 May 2018. https://www.youtube.com/watch?v=VYOjWnS4cMY.

Kaplan, Ilana. "The Hidden References in Childish Gambino's 'This Is America.'" *The Independent,* 11 May 2018, www.independent.co.uk/arts-entertainment/music/features/childish-gambino-donald-glover-this-is-america-hidden-references-music-video-a8342031.html.

Shamsian, Jacob. "24 Things You May Have Missed in Childish Gambino's "This Is America" Music Video." *Business Insider,* 9 May 2018, www.businessinsider.com/this-is-america-music-video-meaning-references-childish-gambino-donald-glover-2018-5#hes-shirtless-for-a-reason-8.

Questions to Consider

1. The text Jacob examined contained a combination of sound, music, and visual information to create an overall message, and rather than analyzing one text or the other (the song or the video) he chose to focus on how all of this information came together into one cohesive text. Looking through this analysis, can you find moments where the strong ethical message of the song/video intersect so that understanding is only possible by examining both? What would be missing if only the song or the video were analyzed, rather than examining them together? How might the meaning of either be misconstrued if they were analyzed as separate texts?

2. Throughout his analysis, Jacob points out the ethical considerations that this multimodal text foregrounds for its audience. While many different approaches could have been taken to this analysis, why might Jacob have chosen to focus on the connections in this text to larger social issues? Why might it be important to seek out and understand social commentaries in music and videos? What can a deep analysis of a text add to our understanding about social injustice or inequities in society?

3. For this analysis, Jacob consulted outside sources to learn more about the text he was analyzing. While this is not always required for a rhetorical analysis, what might it add to understand more about the context or contents of a text? What other kinds of information about a text might be helpful for understanding how it works rhetorically? Why is it important to think about the text itself *and* the context in which it arises?

Hope for a Nation: A Rhetorical Analysis of Barack Obama's 2004 DNC Speech

Nick Viola
Honorable Mention for Rhetorical Analysis

Reflection

I was fortunate enough to be able to choose from a list of provided topics for this paper. Coming up with topics for papers is something I struggle with, as was true later in the semester when doing a research-based argument paper. For this Rhetorical Analysis, I chose Barack Obama's 2004 Democratic National Convention speech because I had never been aware of it, despite my interest in would-be President Obama. I found it challenging navigating my rhetorical analysis of this amazing speech without including the context surrounding Barack Obama that we have all come to know but didn't exist at the time. It was also interesting for me given that I hadn't been born yet when this speech was made. I was able to work through this challenge, as well as later revising my paper with the help of my dad, who provided some insight into the political environment at the time of the speech.

I really pride myself on the way I set myself up to write papers like this. It starts with an outline, organized like my notes, with headers and indentations for new thoughts. I'm able to add simple thoughts or sentences when I feel inspired and include my detailed notes on the speech itself for summaries and quotations. With so much material already organized in an outline, it makes it much easier to overcome the daunting task of starting a paper from page one by cleaning up and completing the work that already exists.

Hope for a Nation: A Rhetorical Analysis of Barack Obama's 2004 DNC Speech

The keynote speech at the Democratic National Convention on July 27, 2004, was given by the relatively unknown Illinois Senator Barack Obama. Unbeknownst to anyone at the time, the young African American politician was about to introduce himself as the future of the Democratic Party, but that was not his intention up on the stage that night. He simply aimed to convey the priorities of the Democratic Party in the upcoming presidential election. In 2004, with a less politically polarized society than we see today, Obama wanted to convey hope for a bright future. The Democratic Party's selling point was the culmination of centuries of civil rights with an all-inclusive democracy; a complete, unified America. A speech with such purpose is littered with deliberate rhetorical techniques, warranting analysis of said rhetoric. By establishing a connection to his audience and purpose, giving profound delivery, exhibiting speech etiquette and word choice, and using deliberate emotional appeals, Barack Obama addressed the American people to outline the Democratic Party's promising future.

Senator Obama opens his speech by addressing the improbability of his presence there that night, gesturing to himself to indicate his race. To elaborate on that remark, he tells the story of his family's history as an example of American optimism. He shares how the meaning of his own name symbolizes his parents' dreams for their son, their legacy carrying through to his own daughters. Following his personal story, the young Senator began to tell the stories of everyday Americans—workers, parents, and students—experiencing unfortunate circumstances beyond their control. These stories are used to plug various Democratic Party policy priorities, and he uses this opportunity to support 2004 Democratic presidential candidate John Kerry, sharing some of Kerry's history and highlighting his service in Vietnam. He connects Kerry to the stories of the citizens he talked about and Democratic campaign issues, putting particular emphasis on the war in Iraq and Afghanistan, after detailing another tale of a young man he met who'd optimistically enlisted. To tie it all together, not-yet-president Obama explicitly expresses hope to inspire the audience: hope for one America, full of equal opportunity and unity against all adversity.

The aforementioned unfamiliarity of people with the young Senator allowed him the opportunity to share his story in a way designed to bind him with the audience, a sort of invented ethos. He tells the story of how his father came to be in America, coming from Kenya on a scholarship with hope for a better life. He highlights his maternal grandparents' service to their country and dreams for their daughter, illustrating them as regular people with big dreams. Barack Obama's story is not unlike that of many Americans, and he points out that his "story is part of the larger American story" (2:45). By sharing it he is able to establish a connection with his audience, as well as the issues he goes on to talk about. He's linked himself to common themes of the American identity, for example the immigrant experience, viewing America as the land of opportunity. He recalls his parents' relationship as an "improbable love … born of two continents" (1:50). Next, he taps into the duty and sacrifice of the WWII generation, his Kansan grandmother working assembly lines and his grandfather enlisting, then coming home and building a life through the GI Bill and FHA. He expresses his belief in America as a place where children can thrive without prejudice holding them back. Finally, he leaves the audience with a memorable moment, a way to refer to the young man they'd never heard of in a way that showed humility and confidence. He calls himself, "a skinny kid with a funny name that believes America has a place for him, too" (14:20).

Though he talks a lot about himself, Obama's speech still promotes Democratic presidential running-mates John Kerry and John Edwards. In addition to his own, the Senator chooses to share some purposeful details about candidate Kerry through the middle of his speech to combat a perceived Republican advantage when it comes to military matters. He reminds the audience that Kerry was once "a young naval lieutenant bravely patrolling the Mekong Delta," (14:13) and is therefore capable of leading America through its newest conflict.

Another sort of situated ethos that cannot be overlooked is the ability to deliver a speech to a live audience. Senator Obama does an incredible job engaging the onlookers, often pausing for emphasis and applause, and of course, when it's convenient to catch his breath. He utilizes hand gestures—literally pointing to a portion of the crowd at one point—to draw in the audience and contribute to flow. He even rhetorically asks the audience whether they "participate in a politics of cynicism or ... in a politics of hope" (13:35). The audience may not be visible in this iteration of the speech, but they are easily heard. Listening to the crowd's reaction illustrates the effectiveness of some of these techniques.

Beyond his captivating delivery, Barack Obama has become known for his carefully choreographed choice of language. He frequently utilizes structure, rhythm, and repetition to emphasize the Democratic Party's values. Obama's repetition is on display as he invites the audience, "tonight, if you feel the same energy that I do, if you feel the same urgency that I do, if you feel the same passion that I do, if you feel the same hopefulness that I do—if we do what we must do" (15:22). Not only does its anaphoric repetition stand out, but this line connects so many aspects of the speech together, showing structure.

His use of repetition is further exemplified when he rhythmically repeats examples of "a child ... who can't read ... a senior citizen ... who can't pay for their prescription," and "an Arab American family" being unfairly "rounded up," all examples that line up with Democratic priorities of education, healthcare, and equality. He declares that those people matter, "even if that's not [our] child ... even if that's not [our] grandparent," and because, "that threatens [our] civil liberties" (11:00–11:30).

For the duration of his speech, Senator Obama uses careful language to avoid directly attacking the Bush administration's conduct of the Iraq and Afghanistan war. A prime example of this comes when he says "we have a solemn obligation not to fudge the numbers or shade the truth about why they're going," and outlines broadly popular priorities such as "caring for the families while they're gone, tending to the soldiers upon their return" and concludes this argument with a powerful statement that America should "never ever go to war without enough troops to win the war, secure the peace, and earn the respect of the world" (9:40–10:05), resulting in one of the loudest applauses of the address.

Much of the emotional appeal throughout the speech comes from stories of people he's met, neighbors and loved ones, fellow Americans going through hard times. From workers losing their union jobs at an industrial plant moving internationally, now competing with their own children for minimum wage jobs, and a father in tears, trying to figure out how to cover his son's medical expenses without health benefits, to a young woman, and so many students like her with the grades and the resolve, but not the money to go to college (4:50–5:25). These stories may be similar to some of those in the audience, or personify their worst fears, but they also have another effect. Obama is trying to create a sense of community responsibility, not to solve these people's problems but to give them equal opportunity to do so. (6:20–6:50). His personal family stories also play into pathos, their big dreams touching the core of many

Americans helped by the idea that "in no other country on earth, is [his] story even possible" (2:50) to appeal to national pride. Later he reminds the audience of the loss of American servicemen and women, and the effects of that on their families. He calls for the discontinuation of partisan and demographic divides, and appeals to unity over military affairs because "there are patriots who opposed the war in Iraq, there are patriots who supported the war in Iraq" (13:00), all to create one "United States of America!" (13:10).

Another tactic for inciting emotional response is citing significant cultural references. Obama quotes the Declaration of Independence's inalienable rights (3:30), an easy way to pull at the heart strings of any proud American. He also alludes to a passage from the Bible's book of Genesis and recites the infamous motto on the United States seal, "e pluribus unum" (11:40–12:00). Both points spark reactions for their religious and national importance. He even calls the present "the crossroads of history" (15:15) to stress the weight of the moment.

Although his immediate audience was in front of him at the Democratic National Convention, Barack Obama effectively addressed the entire nation. He presented the ideals of the Democratic Party, utilizing numerous strategies of ethos, delivery, and pathos to do so. Analyzing this speech from two decades prior proves difficult given the additional history that now surrounds the former Senator, but his words have stood the test of time. Not only is his speech an excellent example of rhetoric, its content can provide a lens through which we can approach similar issues today. Despite the plea toward a hopeful future made in 2004, we find ourselves in an increasingly polarized political environment. However, if we continue to practice hope, putting an emphasis on conversation and community, we may "still come together as a single American family" (11:50).

Work Cited

Obama, Barack. "Obama's 2004 DNC Keynote Speech." *YouTube,* uploaded by CNN, 27 July 2016, https://www.youtube.com/watch?v=ueMNqdB1QIE.

Questions to Consider

1. Analyzing political speeches is an important application of rhetorical analysis skills, as these persuasive texts often have huge effects on national policy, elections, and social identities. What rhetorical work does a political address like this do? Why do politicians attempt to create identification with an audience or tell personal stories, either of themselves or others? How would you compare or contrast the speech Nick has analyzed with other political speeches you have heard?

2. Nick noted that it was challenging to analyze this particular speech without taking into consideration that Obama would later become president. How can understanding the historic moment in a text arises be important for understanding or analyzing that text? Why does the occasion for the speech matter for understanding it? How might the exigence and kairotic moment for the delivery of this speech have influenced what was included or excluded?

3. Although not the primary focus on this analysis, many of the rhetorical moves described by Nick in this paper help create a particular ethos for Obama. Even without seeing this speech yourself, what kind of ethos does Obama display in this speech? How might that have contributed to his successful run for president later? What can you discern about "presidential ethos" from reading this analysis?

Category: Narrative and Reflection

In your first-year writing courses, you may be assigned some type of Narrative or Reflection. While there are different versions of this assignment, these genres typically rely upon personal experience, story, and writing in first person where you address your audience as "I." Unlike more formal academic writing, narratives may use vivid description and words that evoke emotion in readers, painting a picture of a situation or feeling so that your readers have the sense of "being there" when you tell your story. Reflections ask you to think about your own experience deeply and analyze it, the way you might do with a text in other assignments, and share your insights with an audience.

Narratives can serve a variety of purposes in ENGL 101 and 115, and assignments involving narrative may vary greatly from class to class. Personal narratives may require you to tell a story of some aspect of your life, place yourself within a certain cultural context, or ask you to examine an important event in your life that has shaped who you are today. A narrative argument uses story to make an argument where the narrative serves as a representative anecdote to illustrate a larger issue and may or may not include outside sources and research. While each of these types of assignments serves a different purpose, in all cases you may use story, description, dialog, and a first-person perspective in your writing.

Reflective writing, on the other hand, asks you to specifically reflect on your own experience in a new way, deeply analyze some aspect of your life, and then share your discoveries with your reader. There are many versions of this type of writing, and, in fact, you have been reading reflective writing all along in this edition of *The Write Path,* as you read the words by the student authors prior to their essays as they reflected on their experiences writing that piece. Reflection is an integral part of the Jesuit educational and philosophical systems since, unless we pause to deeply reflect on our own experiences or learning, it is easy to miss the important lessons we might learn through this act of reflection.

The following essays offer unique perspectives on subjects ranging from self-expression, family relationships, and the importance of artistic expression and are especially impactful due to the first-person, engaging style that characterizes narrative writing. Throughout your time at Xavier, you, like these authors, might also find that narratives are an effective way to share personal stories that might not otherwise receive much attention in society.

The D'Artagnan Award winner for the Narrative and Reflection category is Samuel Dean for his essay "Introvert or Stolen Words?" This narrative, which reflects on the origins of the writer's introversion, utilizes vivid details, metaphor, and evocative sensory information to create a story that has a clear point, purpose, and implications. Our judges thought that the structure of this story was extremely compelling and left a lasting impression, and said that the content is "poignant and evocative, using language, imagery, and details well to convey a complex idea." As you read, be aware of the details Samuel uses to tell this story, as well as your reaction to them.

The next essay, "Now He's 6 Feet Tall," is by Carolyn Isaly. In a story about both figurative and literal growth, this author's essay is subtle and poignant, offering a perspective that is likely relatable in some way to many students. Our judges said that Carolyn's story is "restrained in a way that first-year writers often don't achieve, and makes smart use of literary devices" that support the tone and structure of this narrative. As you read, think about the way that the author uses metaphor and details to engage the reader.

The final essay in this category is Aidan Oke's "Why We Should Ban Drag Bans!" This piece combines a personal story with research to create a compelling narrative argument that is well written and makes a convincing case for why banning drag is detrimental. The writer's personal experience bookends this essay, and our judges said that it is "a great example of how personal stories, experience, and empathy matter when making an argument." Aidan's essay also carries the D'Artagnan Insignia for Advocacy in Action, as it promotes expression that is often culturally suppressed or marginalized. As you read this essay, notice how personal story works alongside traditional argumentation and clearly articulates the ethical stance taken by the author.

In your ENGL 101 or 115 classes, you may have the opportunity to write a narrative, narrative argument, or reflection of some kind, and while your particular assignment may differ from these examples, there are still guidelines of effective storytelling that you can take away from these essays. As you read, notice how the students tell their stories—what details they give, how you react or feel when you read, and the effects of their descriptions—and then remember these concepts when you craft your own narratives or reflections. We all tell stories in our lives every day, whether as an official assignment or not. Storytelling is an important aspect of culture and social interaction, and learning to craft an effective narrative as part of your writing gives you the opportunity to share your experiences with wider audiences.

Introvert or Stolen Words?

Samuel Dean
D'Artagnan Award Winner for Narrative or Reflection

Reflection

This idea came to me mid-class after Dr. Nieto said, "think of something that has built your character." This prompt resonated with me. Then, with some soul searching, I was able to write something vulnerable. The most challenging part is writing about yourself while being neutral, guiding the reader to side with you without being too biased. I revised this piece with Dr. Nieto. The best advice is that writing is a part of you that you allow others to read. Write what inspires you, and don't be scared. It can be fun to just let the ink flow.

Introvert or Stolen Words?

My biggest question over my first four months of college is how I became an introvert. To be completely honest, I'm not a hundred percent sure, but it started just before Manresa, the event where you must be social. It wasn't a fast change either. I slowly stopped wanting to hang out and be in big settings, and this feeling of pure terror filled my soul when I had to go out in public.

I used to be able to sing in front of others on a stage with the big yellow spotlight glistening on the sweat on my forehead and showing every single imperfection on me and my makeup, but it never seemed to bother me. Maybe it's because I'm talking to them, and they don't have to speak to me. Besides the point, it seems to stem from my childhood, like most of my problems.

It was a Tuesday at 3 pm. I was 8. I had come home, and I already felt the same soul-swallowing anxiety I get now. The house was not a home but a haunted one; darkness filled every corner, and the bitterness was cold enough to give you goosebumps. No one was home other than my sisters and me.

By 6 o'clock, Mom made dinner, and my family was sitting down and ready to eat when I realized something was wrong. No one said a word since my parents got home. As the steam rolled off the spaghetti, the house was so quiet you could hear the crickets popping their popcorn as if they had paid for the best seats to a UFC match.

Like usual, Mom said in this fake happy tone, "What was the best part of your day, Sam?" I don't remember what I said, although I do remember her not saying anything to my father.

As dinner finished up, the sink sounded like a light waterfall. Then I heard Mom fully release the fake happy voice; this was pure anger. Screams filled the house as the kids went to their rooms. The fighting was a nightly occasion, and we all knew the drill at this point, almost like a tornado siren. Something was different this time; this wasn't just a warning. Little did we know our house would be torn to shreds within minutes.

The war started once the kids were in their bedrooms, and neither party was leaving until they won. 9 o'clock arrived, and I walked to my parent's bedroom with fear in my heart; all I hear is BANG. My dad had punched the wall trying to reach my mom, who had locked herself in the bathroom. Blood poured from my father's knuckles, and my mom screamed with terror. He hit the wood stud. I needed to step in; I needed to save my mom, but the words from my mouth dissipated. "Right here, right now. Right here, right now. Right here, right now." I said in my mind. I needed to speak, and for the first time, I realized I had lost control over my words. With my power stripped from my soul, I walked back to my room with horror-filled eyes because I had just walked up to the tornado and watched everything in my life get pulled apart.

10 o'clock, and everyone hears a SLAM. The echo of the slamming door filled the cold house. My father had left. No side won this war, and the bystanders were distraught. Blood stained the carpet; tears filled our eyes like an infinity pool. The kids watched the tornado rip through the house and leave. The worst part, it wasn't over.

In the following two years, the divorce and the effects of my father filled the empty corners of the house, and my war had begun: a war with myself. My father tried to take everything from us; he only succeeded in taking my words.

I have always seen, or until now seen, myself as an extrovert, always making friends and trying to hang out with friends—the loss of words also transferred over to my friends. I couldn't talk, so as a result, as soon as I would hang out with them, it would feel like life got drained out of me like a boring class; all I could do was watch the clock until it was over. Soon, I would stop asking to hang out with people, and they would stop inviting me. No one wanted to be with someone who couldn't wait to go home.

Losing control over our words is a feeling we all know: lips vacuum sealed shut and everything to say and no chance you can say it.

Or the words spill out at once, and everything's being said with no chance you can stop it. It's a feeling of power being stripped from everything in your body, and it is terrifying. We all have experiences that make us who we are, genuinely shaping us into who we are supposed to become. So maybe it's not being an introvert; maybe it's just learning how to reopen myself to others.

Questions to Consider

1. Samuel uses figurative language in his essay, describing sensory input from his surroundings in the past. What do you picture in your mind when you hear the descriptions of the surroundings in which the main part of this story takes place? What senses are invoked through these descriptions? What is the purpose of describing a scene using multiple senses in a narrative such as this?

2. In this essay, Samual uses the metaphor of a tornado to describe the action and its effects. What feelings or images does a tornado potentially evoke in a reader? What rhetorical work does a sustained metaphor do within this story? What other metaphors might be applicable for a story like this?

3. In narrative or reflective writing, it is sometimes possible to make connections to readers in ways that are not so apparent in conventional academic essays. How does Samuel make connections to readers throughout this piece? How can reading about someone else's experience or life potentially affect readers? Can you make any connections between Samuel's story and your own life, or the lives of others around you?

Now He's 6 Feet Tall

Carolyn Isaly
Honorable Mention for Narrative or Reflection

Reflection

When my freshman Rhetoric professor assigned our class the Personal Narrative assignment, I was pretty nervous. I did not know what exactly I wanted to focus on or a direction I wanted to take the paper. My process for finding a topic started with me simply thinking of what was happening in my life. I had recently gone home and was completely startled by my younger brother being taller than me. When actually writing the assignment, I reflected on my experience going home over winter break and wrote short paragraphs regarding specific details I remembered. I then went to the Writing Center where I got help refining my paper and reordering the paragraphs. Before going to the Writing Center, I was not planning on including a section from my own experience and thoughts in the past, but I really think it added to the piece. My advice would be, whatever topic you choose, try to think about other points of view and possibly views of a younger version of yourself. Do not be limited by the event itself, think about all aspects of it, and all the sides. Also don't feel pressured to write the paper in order. Moving things around and writing when you think of details can improve the quality of your writing.

Now He's 6 Feet Tall

Rocco was born 1,164 days after the greatest day ever recorded … the day I was born. He weighed 10 pounds 5 ounces and was 23.5 inches long—about 4 inches longer than average, so it was evident from his very first breath that he was not going to be a small individual. I, however, for the majority of my life, chose to ignore this fact. It wasn't until I was 17 years old that my years of taller, older sibling ignorant bliss came to an end.

That particular afternoon, Rocco sat on the couch perpendicular to the one I was sitting on in the living room. We liked to sit this way—close enough that I could cover his ears and usher him out of the room if need be, but far enough away that he felt independent.

To be honest, I don't remember what show I had turned on the TV. I know that the show was loud, with explosions blasting out of the speakers. Rocco loved anything with explosions. My plan was that it would serve as a distraction from the exclamations my mother was furiously forcing into her phone just a few feet behind us in the kitchen.

"IT'S MY WEEKEND WITH THE KIDS!" My mother shouted as she paced back and forth between the sink and the refrigerator.

I glanced over at Rocco, grasping to the hope that he would be unable to hear anything other than the BOOM from the TV that not only rang in my ears, but physically shook me in my seat. Just looking at Rocco you could tell that my plan was not working. His eyes darted back and forth between the TV screen and the kitchen. His left leg was shaking to the point that his head bobbed up and down just a bit.

I used to sit there like that when I was even younger than him. The shaking and the yelling had found harmony back then. They happened separately, but seemed to make more sense together, like my leg was made to shake at the sound of the yelling.

Unlike Rocco (and most kids for that matter) I could never even pretend to pay attention to the TV. I would be too focused on my mother. Her short, thick brown hair that she always had braided down the middle. Her beautiful, dark eyes that she never let shed a tear. Back then my dad would be in the kitchen with her. Yelling. They were always yelling. Not around Rocco though. Never around Rocco. I wouldn't let them.

You're not that little girl anymore. Take care of Rocco. I reminded myself. He is too small to be able to handle this. You have to be there for him.

In an attempt to take control of the situation, I rose to my feet and stared at him until he did the same, but something felt off.

It was Rocco standing in the living room with me. It had to be. This man looming before me was wearing Rocco's dark blue Nike hat that he refused to take off, and had on his classic black T-shirt that read "Don't Interrupt Me While I'm Gaming" in large neon green lettering. It was Rocco I assured myself, but it also wasn't. His back stood tall, no hunch to be detected. His long legs broke the barrier of the pant leg so a significant amount of his lower calf was visible. In awe I faced him, and for the first time as I did so, his eyes were looking down on me. I was not watching over him.

He began to walk towards the stairs that led to our respective bedrooms. The first step creaked under the weight of his foot, and mine did the same as I walked up behind him. As I opened my bedroom door, I took one last glance behind me to watch Rocco walk into his room down the hall. Realistically there's no way this could have happened, but I swear I saw him duck as he stepped through the doorway.

All the blinds were shut in my room, and I didn't think to turn the light on before I laid down on the bed. I allowed the blankets, sheets, and pillows to engulf me as I stared at the ceiling.

I felt lighter. It was almost as if the weight of the shield I had forged myself into had withered away.

Trying to protect Rocco from my family felt like being trapped in an elevator. The longer you are entrapped, the less air there is surrounding you. I started to take fewer and shorter breaths in order to allow him to survive. Rocco was taller now though. Older. Stronger. I could now allow myself to step out of the elevator and breathe. In and out. In and out. Deep breaths that filled my lungs beyond what I had ever imagined. Deep breaths that I took all for myself without feeling like I was inhibiting anyone else from breathing. I was finally free not only to breathe, but to live my life for myself.

I ran to Rocco's bedroom, my mind completely stress free for the first time since I could remember. I didn't even think to knock as I pushed the door of his bedroom open, almost slipping on a pile of Legos he conveniently had on the floor as I continued to rush towards him.

"What the heck?" Rocco says to me confused as I force my arms around him.

"Just let me hold my big, little brother for a second."

Questions to Consider

1. In her reflection, Carolyn mentions taking her essay to the Writing Center and rearranging the structure of her story based on feedback. Looking at the organization of the story now, how is it arranged? How might it have been arranged differently? Can you think of other structural choices a writer can make when conveying a story that happened in the past?

2. Carolyn also mentioned that she added details to this story that expressed her thoughts in the past. How does sharing her past thoughts add layers and perspectives to this story? How do imagination, memory, and details come together to create a compelling story? How can writers decide what to include and exclude when telling a narrative based on real-life events?

3. This narrative uses effective metaphors and sensory details to convey ideas. How many rhetorical devices like these can you find in Carolyn's essay? What purpose do they serve for the reader? What response did you have to these techniques when you read her story for the first time?

Why We Should Ban Drag Bans!

Aidan Oke
Honorable Mention for Narrative or Reflection

Reflection

When my teacher told us that we were writing a narrative argument for our first essay, there were a lot of varying ideas that ran through my head. I wanted to use my writing to call attention to a social justice issue that is beginning to reach its peak because of the upcoming election. I wanted to use the experiences of individuals in the LGBTQ+ community to educate people on the rise of drag bans which is a problem that has not gotten a lot of attention beyond the queer community itself. One of the most daunting challenges I faced while writing was finding sources that could be easily applied to the topic I was focusing on. Due to the recency of current drag bans, there are not many detailed sources or peer-reviewed articles to choose from. However, because of how my teacher planned our classes, I was given many tools to work with and plenty of time to do detailed research. Being able to sort information from my sources into charts was one of the best crutches I had while writing and whenever I did not know what to put next, I could go back to my chart. It's also much easier to organize an essay when you can fit every sentence into a category like a fact or commentary.

My suggestion to any incoming writers is to listen and find importance in what you're writing. By paying attention to feedback that you're given from both instructors and peers, you will be able to find flaws in your writing that you may not notice otherwise. When you are writing about something important to you, it is much easier to come up with ideas and concepts for what to put on paper. While writing this piece, I would come up with new ideas no matter where I was. I would write on napkins in the cafeteria or put phrases in my notes app to use later. This is because I was writing about something that mattered to me.

Why We Should Ban Drag Bans!

On the night of my eighteenth birthday, my friend and I went to a small local LGBTQ+ club that was in our city. I had stopped celebrating birthdays and the year prior my time was spent lying in bed and watching cheesy Netflix shows. This particular night though, my friend insisted I celebrate my birthday by doing one of the only things an eighteen-year-old gains from their new age; going to whatever club that allowed people below drinking age inside to see drag shows.

This was my first time interacting with drag and I was fascinated. This queen was a local artist and wore a shimmering red sequin dress that night. The light bounced off the dress and lit up the audience and the song she lip-synced to was slow and calming. At the end of this song, she talked about her story; outside of drag, she was a trans woman with a husband and kids. She talked about the drag bans sweeping through some states and how these bans disproportionally damage the trans community. These laws proposed that dressing in clothes that were not associated with the gender you were assigned at birth would be illegal. Original drag laws required that people had to have 3–5 articles of clothing that would typically be associated with their assigned gender, but these laws ultimately come down to the opinion of whomever is enforcing them. With too much room for discrimination, trans people and drag queens alike would have to be afraid of walking down the street in the clothes that make them comfortable. Drag bans do not just affect performers—they affect the entire queer community. Drag itself is rich in culture and an important part of queer history. Banning drag is unconstitutional and denies children of the many positive effects of being exposed to drag.

Often, the main argument that is heard in favor of banning drag is that it endangers children by exposing them to things that are perverse and inappropriate. However, exposing children to things that are different and new to them is a positive way to foster growth. In an interview conducted by Eric Pinckney, he talks to a New Jersey native queen and host of her local "drag queen story hour." Miss Savannah Georgia expresses that people should be exposing children to love, acceptance, and compassion because learning important lessons at a young age is the best time for someone to grow. From the outside looking in, it may be difficult for someone to understand the influence drag has on queer culture, but if children are educated on these topics early, they will grow to have a better understanding of LGBTQ+ individuals and for some children being exposed to queer culture may help them feel more comfortable with accepting their identities in their teen years. According to licensed clinical social worker Jennifer Stallbaumer Rouyer, encouraging kids to be curious, confident, and kind starts with accepting diversity and inclusion; the best way to do this is for kids to be introduced to a variety of communities and opportunities by their parents. Going to places like drag queen story hours is a healthy way to carefully introduce kids to queer culture without being over-stimulating or confusing. Many children who attend are there for the enchanting stories and colorful dresses, which allows them to build a tolerance for queer culture in a fun and engaging way. There are so many positive aspects to drag that children would be denied access to because of drag bans.

Although the benefits drag brings are important, it should also be taken into consideration that banning drag would be a complete violation of constitutional rights. Robert Wolf, who has covered issues with Congress and the Whitehouse for over 30 years, states in an article that art, music, and clothes are covered under the First Amendment promise of free speech. The Constitution was made to give the American people the rights that they deserve, and by looking only at the surface level of the term "free speech," we are doing an injustice to the people who are supposed to be protected by the First Amendment. Free speech is not limited to what we say—it also covers how we express ourselves in day-to-day life. Reporter Syndey Kashiwagi reports about a decision made on April 1, 2023, from U.S. District Court Judge Thomas Parker, who was appointed by Donald Trump during his presidency, agreeing that banning drag was unconstitutional. Parker stated that the law that was trying to be passed in Tennessee was a restriction on speech that was based on a one-sided viewpoint and that the law itself was too broad. Although this only temporarily blocked the law that is trying to be passed in Tennessee, it should set a precedent for how anti-drag laws are viewed because it is important to acknowledge the need for queer expression. Even though drag is foreign to some people, it has existed for a long time and has only recently become a target for these laws. If we throw the Constitution aside when trying to pass laws, no matter what those laws are meant to address, it sets a bad example for our country and demonstrates a lack of care for Americans as a whole.

Ultimately the drag bans being pushed in many states across America are not having the impact they are meant to have. It is completely reasonable to want to protect children from something that at first glance does not seem safe. However, in attempting to keep drag away from kids, these laws will deny them the important lessons about love and acceptance that come hand-in-hand with drag and would violate our constitutional right to free speech as well. When I was eighteen, I was introduced to drag for the very first time. I left that show with a story about a woman who was scared for not only the livelihood of her career, but also for her kids, her husband, and herself. So when I think about protecting queer art, I do not just think about saving drag shows from being banned. I also think about protecting people like that beautiful woman I saw on stage that night and protecting the children waiting for her at home that she spoke about with so much passion and love. That is why I will never stop protecting queer art.

Works Cited

Kashiwagi, Sydney. "Trump-appointed Federal Judge Rules Tennessee's Anti-Drag Show Law is 'Unconstitutional.'" *CNN*, https://www.cnn.com/2023/06/03/politics/tennessee-drag-ban-law-unconstitutional/index.html.

Pinckney, Eric. "Drag Isn't Dangerous for Children, but Drag-Bans Are." *USA Today*, https://www.usatoday.com/story/opinion/voices/2023/07/03/anti-drag-laws-harm-kids-lgbtq-community/70347476007/.

Stallbaumer, Jennifer and Patricia A. Davis. "How to Promote Diversity and Inclusion in Your Child's Life." *Childrens Mercy Kansas City*, https://www.childrensmercy.org/parent-ish/2021/09/diversity/.

Wolf, Robert. "What The First Amendment Protects – And What it Doesn't." *USA Today*, https://www.usatoday.com/story/news/politics/2018/04/06/what-first-amendment-protects-and-what-doesnt/469920002/.

Questions to Consider

1. A narrative argument begins with a story and often allows the story to carry most of the weight of the argument, though it may also include outside sources. As a reader, which parts of this argument were the most convincing or compelling to you? How did you react to the story at the beginning and end of this piece as compared to the center research-based paragraphs? What rhetorical work does narrative have in conjunction with more classic forms of argumentation?

2. In his reflection, Aidan stresses the importance of writing about issues that are meaningful, and the essay itself articulates a commitment to writing about protecting queer art. How is this different from essays that try to maintain "a neutral stance," even if they are clearly taking a side? How might the genre for this essay allow space to clearly articulate one's position in ways that traditional essays might not? What are the affordances and constraints of a narrative argument as a genre?

3. Aidan's essay is based in personal experience and inspired by identity in part of a particular community. How does knowing about first-hand experience construct Aidan's ethos in this essay? What rhetorical work does stating his dedication to an important issue do for Aidan's argument? What might story-telling and empathy add to the art of argumentation?

Category: Multimodal Composing

Multimodal argumentation describes any artifact that uses "multiple modes" of communication, such as text, image, sound, music, video, etc. to communicate a persuasive message to a particular audience. Once you consider it, you realize that many persuasive artifacts are already multimodal—even an image with a text caption is multimodal. In fact, this genre may be one that you are already very familiar with in your daily life, as most digital texts combine multiple modes of communication together to create more effective, engaging messages than text alone can offer by itself.

Because multimodal texts are so prevalent, it is important to learn how to analyze, interact with, and create these works yourself, which is why some type of multimodal project will be required in all of your first-year writing courses. While there is significant intellectual work that goes into these projects—as much or perhaps even more than in traditional text-based works—students often find these projects to be engaging and fun. Multimodality can allow you to integrate more creative methods of expressing your ideas, persuading an audience, or demonstrating your research-based knowledge than a traditional paper. Multimodal projects may be assigned alongside, or as part of, a longer research process that may include a traditional research-based argument paper, or you may even "remediate" a text-based paper that you wrote by transforming your work into a multimodal version of the same argument.

As you can imagine, there are nearly limitless possibilities for the parameters and mediums of a multimodal project. However your particular course approaches multimodality, you will still be asked to consider how the modes of communication interact with one another, what effects these mediums may have upon your audience, and what affordances and constraints are inherent in the modes of communication that you use. Multimodality opens up new ways to communicate that can reach wider public audiences than traditional academic essays can, so this type of assignment may also help you practice creating arguments and messages that can be used to intervene in larger public forums.

Our D'Artagnan Award winner for Multimodal Composing is Jamie Swisshelm for their song "The Way to Freedom." This project is an excellent example of how an argument can be "remediated" and shows how a message can be transformed to reach a wider audience. In this case, Jamie started with a Proposal Argument entitled, "Making Rainbow Dreams Come True: Queer Representation in College Theatre," and wrote a song that effectively communicates the main purpose of that argument into the medium of song. In their reflection, Jamie discusses the process by which they composed the multimodal argument and also expresses how first-year writing projects can be utilized to promote issues that students care about and can draw experience from the different communities in which students are involved. Judges found Jamie's project "delightful, both in terms of message and execution" and thought that they did a great job of "showing how a similar message can be put into another format to reach a wider or different audience." Because this work promotes social justice and inclusion, in addition to winning the D'Artagnan Award, it has also earned the D'Artagnan Insignia for Advocacy in Action. Jamie's lyrics are included in the following pages along with a link to the video on YouTube, and the Proposal Argument and song are also featured on *The Write Path* 9th Edition Multimodal Argument website (see QR code below).

The next piece is Nadia Leontescu's research poster entitled "Juul Really Isn't Cool: The Dangers of DNA Damage from E-Cigarette Use." The medium of a research poster is often used to present scholarly work and research in venues such as conferences. Judges found Nadia's poster to be "an excellent example of how a research poster can display a condensed, visually appealing argument that connects immediately to viewers" and described it as a "professional-looking poster [that] would be appropriate for a conference display or talk." Learning to communicate research-based arguments to multiple audiences is one of the goals of first-year writing classes, and this exemplary model of a multimodal assignment is one that you might be asked to do in other upper-level courses as you continue with your education at Xavier.

The third piece included in this category is called "The Lasting Effects of the Foster System" by Ebony Billups. This photo essay uses images to help readers connect to the humanity of the people affected by this issue, and because of that, it also carries the D'Artagnan Insignia for Advocacy in Action. The personal narrative as a multimodal argument can be very persuasive to readers, and our judges noted that Ebony's work "evokes empathy and challenges readers to look at this issue from the point of view of those who are actually affected." While we often think of college essays as being without images or pictures, this multimodal composition shows how images can remind us that human beings are affected strongly by separation and trauma, a rhetorical appeal that is harder to communicate in words alone.

As you can see from this selection of multimodal projects, there is quite a wide variety of options when it comes to projects like this. How you engage with multimodality will vary from class to class, and as you gain experience analyzing and creating multimodal compositions, you can expand your skills and ability to communicate across diverse public audiences. Because multimodal texts are so prevalent in our world, these skills can help you as you move forward in your college career and allow you to create messages that can be distributed well beyond a classroom setting.

The Writing Program maintains a Sharepoint site to store these projects. To access them, you can scan the QR code below or type in the URL—your professor may also provide a direct link for you in class or in Canvas. (To see additional projects, once you are on the Sharepoint site, you can click the "Pages" link to see work from previous years.)

Here is the link to the Sharepoint site: *https://myxavier. sharepoint.com/sites/WritePath*

Or scan this QR code to view *The Write Path 9th* edition Sharepoint site:

The Way to Freedom

Jamie Swisshelm
D'Artagnan Award Winner for Multimodal Composing

Medium

Song, Video, Proposal Argument

Reflection

In my English Composition class, we wrote a Proposal Argument that challenged us to look at a community we are a part of, find a problem within that community and propose potential solutions for it. I combined two communities that I am very actively a part of—the LGBTQ+ community and the theatre community—and researched the benefits of queer representation in the college theatre space. Our professor then asked us to revise our Proposal Argument into a Multimodal Argument, and immediately the idea of a song came to mind. I am a songwriter, and utilizing a medium that I am familiar with would help effectively convey the point of the argument, as well as emphasize the importance of said point.

The challenges of this project came in the early stages, as it always does with writing songs. The first step is always the hardest. A song can spark from anywhere—the melody, the words, the accompaniment, etc. Having so many avenues to pick can be overwhelming. Typically, my writing process waits for inspiration to strike before I can get going, but with a project with a deadline, I couldn't wait for that inspiration to strike; I had to just do it.

With this song, the first thing that came to me was the chord progression. Once I had that down, I wrote out my first draft of the lyrics. After revising the lyrics for a day or two, I found a day where I had a couple hours of free time and recorded everything, from my ukulele to my vocals. After recording everything, I spent around two hours on post-production, which is honestly not a lot of time. I then had to take my audio file, tack it into my video editing software and make it into a presentable YouTube video, which took another thirty minutes.

Writing a song for class instead of writing a paper is not something I am unfamiliar with. I've done this in high school as well, and it's got its pros and cons. Writing a paper comes easily to me once I lock in, but it's usually once I'm pushed to the wall with deadlines. With writing a song, it was easier to get started earlier and I had the passion for it, but I can't say it was easier overall than a traditional paper. It hard to revise a song once it's locked in and recorded, so most of my revising was for the earlier stages of the project. I revised lyrics over and over until they were final. I experimented a bit during post-production with sounds that I wanted in my song, and if they didn't fit, I scrapped it and tried again. Songwriting is a lot of trial and error, so perseverance is crucial.

As well as you can within the confines of your project, find something that is interesting to write about. It is so much harder to find passion for writing and improve your skills if you aren't motivated by your topic.

The Way to Freedom

They push us down so we won't scream
They silence us so we won't reveal their scheme
The world is not in black and white
We're here and queer and we will fight
To paint our world in reds and golds and greens

So put us up on the stages
'Cause we're writing pages
In the history books
Our names are engraved
They'll always know that we have paved
The way to freedom

They're trying to take away our power
But day by day and hour by hour
We're building ourselves up again
We have ideas and we will win
Gardens aren't beautiful without the flowers

So put us up on the stages
'Cause we're writing pages
In the history books
Our names are engraved
They'll always know that we have paved
The way to freedom

We won't compromise ourselves to fit your vision
Of what the world should be
Music, theatre and artists made the decision
To amplify the voices of you and me
Whoa, whoa

So put us up on the stages, yeah (Yeah, yeah, yeah)
'Cause we're writing pages (We're writing pages)
In the history books
Our names are engraved
They'll always know that we have paved
The way to freedom
The way to freedom
Whoa

Link to song on YouTube: *https://youtu.be/ceHZCm7p4Qo*

Here is the link to the Sharepoint site: *https://myxavier. sharepoint.com/sites/WritePath*

Or scan this QR code to view *The Write Path* 9th edition Sharepoint site:

Questions to Consider

1. Arguments come in many forms and mediums. Can you think of a song, poem, film, or other work of art that you found persuasive in your own life? How can music or other art forms connect with audiences in ways that may be different from a written text? What might be a benefit of "remediating" an argument into a new multimodal format?

2. In their reflection, Jamie said that their song was another way to "effectively convey the point of the argument [in the Proposal Argument] as well as emphasize the importance of said point." When you read the original argument and listen to the song, what connections can you make about the main point of that argument? Which aspects do you find the most compelling? Are there areas where the text-based argument is more convincing? Or the song? If you were trying to get a point across to a wide audience, how might you utilize multiple modes of argumentation to do that?

3. All arguments utilize various rhetorical strategies in order to be persuasive. What rhetorical appeals or devices do you see at work in Jamie's song? Are those similar to, or different from, the essay on which the song was based? What appeals do you think are most important or effective in creative works like this? Are there some rhetorical appeals, strategies, or devices that might be easier or more difficult to enact in a song versus an essay?

Juul Really Isn't Cool: The Dangers of DNA Damage from E-Cigarette Use

Nadia Leontescu
Honorable Mention for Multimodal Composing

Medium

Research Poster

Reflection

The whole idea of creating this research poster was to create a multimodal work out of a research paper. However, if I'm being completely honest, remediating my research paper into the poster was difficult. Knowing that I was presenting the poster helped a bit, but there was just so much research and information that I wanted to convey that it felt grueling to have to cut most of it out for the poster. However, I knew that getting the key points and the entire why of my research was the most important parts to include, so that is exactly what I did. Since my paper was very biologically focused, the poster provided an opportunity to really hit the 'why does it matter?' home. I could discuss what I found from studies and the processes that occur through a presentation—which is easier to convey through speech anyway—so I essentially used my topic sentences plus some of the broader research to formulate the 'body' of the poster. The visuals were key, especially since I couldn't put any in my paper, so I used the sources I already read through and utilized for evidence to obtain graphs and other visuals.

From there, it was all about formatting and making the poster appealing. I think turning my paper into a poster helped me reshape my argument to even more of a general audience-type presentation. It got me to really recognize that I will be talking to peers about this complicated, very 'sciencey' topic so I need to tone down the jargon and focus on explaining the important terms. This also helped me shape a new argument that is focused on the future and the implications of my research versus just what I can argue/prove with studies and papers. By taking this route of the argument, my peers not only see why it's important to discuss this, but also to influence their interest on the topic. I'm interested in all the biological processes and studies; however, that is not everyone's cup of tea. So, focusing on implications can spark interest for those who don't necessarily care about all the science behind it.

Juul Really Isn't Cool: The Dangers of DNA Damage from E-Cigarette Use

(A condensed preview of Nadia's research poster.)

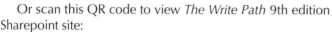

For a full-color enlarged view of the research poster, please visit the Sharepoint site: *https://myxavier.sharepoint.com/sites/WritePath*

Or scan this QR code to view *The Write Path* 9th edition Sharepoint site:

Questions to Consider

1. As mentioned in the introduction to this section, all mediums contain affordances and constraints on what can be said or expressed, and Nadia mentioned in her reflection that it was challenging to condense the information from her argument into the poster. What affordances and constraints are part of a research poster? What can someone "do" in a poster that might be harder in an essay?

2. Research posters are a common way that scholars present their work to colleagues, especially in certain disciplines. What kinds of information do you think would work best in this format? Are there topics, disciplines, information, or situations where a research poster might be particularly effective? How is a research poster different from, or similar to, mediums like infographics? How could a research poster be adapted for different audiences or purposes?

3. Sometimes scholars present posters at conferences for work that is in progress or that they are still analyzing. Nadia also mentioned in her reflection that she used her topic sentences to create the body of the poster. We often think of presentations as the final step of a research process, but could it also be utilized at different points in research? Can you imagine a way to use a research poster as an outlining or invention tool? What elements of a research poster might facilitate organization, clarifying main points, or garnering feedback on research?

The Lasting Effects of the Foster System

Ebony Billups
Honorable Mention for Multimodal Composing

Medium

Photo Essay/Narrative Argument

Reflection

When considering what to submit for this project, I decided that I wanted to write about something that meant a great deal to me. Writing this essay, I knew that I wanted it to bring attention to an issue often overlooked.

While writing a multimodal essay was refreshing in the sense that I didn't have to rely solely on my use of words to convey my emotions and message to my audience, it was also extremely challenging. I'd never written a piece like this before, and given all of the issues my family and I faced with the system, I had a lot more to talk about than what was noted here. Writing this essay meant making a sacrifice—the draft and revision process was no cakewalk. One major issue is that I wanted to bring up every important point, but I could not include all the things I wanted to talk about. I had to realize that to make my argument, I needed to write about fewer points to make the essay more digestible and coherent.

Despite the challenges that I faced writing and rewriting this essay, it was still a great experience. If I had to give advice to first year writers, I would say two things, the first being to write about what speaks to you most. I found that writing essays can be an expression of your inner self, the page a stage for you to speak on something that first spoke to you once. The second piece of advice is that before you write your essay, especially if you're passionate about it, take your time. Know how you want to structure your argument and what's most important to drive your point!

The Lasting Effects of the Foster System

(A preview of Ebony's Photo Essay/Narrative Argument.)

The Foster Care System: Destruction and Separation of Families

Here is the link to the Sharepoint site: *https://myxavier.share-point.com/sites/WritePath*

Or scan this QR code to view *The Write Path* 9th edition Sharepoint site:

Questions to Consider

1. In her reflection, Ebony mentions how difficult it was to make choices about what to include and exclude in her argument to make it more coherent and accessible to her audience. How do you decide what to include and exclude in an argument, especially one that you know a lot about? What are some strategies for figuring out what and how much an audience needs to know? What could be the downside of giving too much information? Or not enough?

2. Ebony mentions that she wrote about something very meaningful to her and she advises other student writers to do the same. How can being passionate about an issue lead to more effective writing? What issues do you care deeply about that you could potentially apply your personal experience and rhetorical skills to persuade others? What are some of the challenges of writing about an issue you care a lot about? What are some of the benefits?

3. This project makes an argument using images and words, but is also largely based in personal experience. How does first-hand experience of an issue affect the ethos of the writer? What kinds of rhetorical appeals do you see at work in this project? How do the images work with the text to be persuasive? How would this piece be different if the words or the images were removed? Can you imagine remediating this argument in another way to reach different audiences?